Recollections
of the late Fleet Admiral

CHESTER W. NIMITZ

as given by his daughter, Miss Nancy Nimitz,
and in conjunction with her mother,
Mrs. Chester W. Nimitz

U. S. Naval Institute
Annapolis, Maryland
1970

Preface

These manuscripts are the result of two tape-recorded interviews with Miss Nancy Nimitz (the second with the assistance of Mrs. Chester Nimitz) in San Francisco, California in June, 1969. They were conducted by John T. Mason, Jr., Director of Oral History for the U. S. Naval Institute.

Only minor emendations and corrections have been made by the participants. The reader is asked therefore to bear in mind the fact that he is reading a transcript of the spoken word rather than the written word.

These interviews are part of a series dealing with the late Fleet Admiral Chester W. Nimitz and were intended for use in the preparation of a biography of the late Fleet Admiral.

DECLARATION OF TRUST

The undersigned does hereby appoint and designate as his (or her) Trustee herein, the Secretary-Treasurer and Publisher of the United States Naval Institute to perform and discharge the following duties, powers, and privileges in connection with the possession and use of a certain taped interview between the undersigned and the Oral History Department of the United States Naval Institute.

(1) As an <u>Open</u> transcript. It may be read (or the tape audited) by qualified researchers upon presentation of proper credentials as determined by the Trustee.

(2) It is expressly understood that in giving this authorization, I am in no way precluded from placing such restrictions as I may desire upon use of the interview at any time during my lifetime, nor does this authorization in any way affect my rights to the copyright of any literary expressions that may be contained in the interview.

Witness my hand and seal this 14th day of November 1969:

_____

I hereby accept and consent to the foregoing Declaration of Trust and the powers therein conferred upon me as Trustee:

_____
Secretary-Treasurer and Publisher

DECLARATION OF TRUST

The undersigned does hereby appoint and designate as his (her) Trustee herein, the Secretary-Treasurer and Publisher of the United States Naval Institute to perform and discharge the following duties, powers, and privileges in connection with the possession and use of a certain taped interview between the undersigned and the Oral History Department of the United States Naval Institute.

(1) As an <u>Open</u> transcript it may be read (or the tape audited) by qualified researchers upon presentation of proper credentials as determined by the Trustee. In the case of interviews about the late Fleet Admiral C. W. Nimitz, it is intended that first use of the material shall be made by the biographer of the Fleet Admiral, Professor E. B. Potter, and the Naval Institute is authorized to deal with the material in this fashion.

(2) It is expressly understood that in giving this authorization, I am in no way precluded from placing such restrictions as I may desire upon use of the interview at any time during my lifetime, nor does this authorization in any way affect my rights to the copyright of any literary expressions that may be contained in the interview.

Witness my hand and seal this __8__ day of __June__ 19__70__

Catherine F. Nimitz

I hereby accept and consent to the foregoing Declaration of Trust and the powers therein conferred upon me as Trustee:

R. E. Bowler
Secretary-Treasurer and Publisher

Interview with Miss Nancy Nimitz in San Francisco, California
By John T. Mason, Jr.
Date: Saturday morning, 7 June 1969

Q: Miss Nancy, how good of you to consent to talk for this tape about your father, your recollections of your father. I expect the best way to do it is to attempt, perhaps, a chronological order, but if you fall from that structure, it will be perfectly all right.

Miss N.: Well, what struck me last night when I sat down with a pad of paper and a pencil and just started jotting down things chronologically was that when I got to the bottom of the page and looked over the sort of key words that I had put down to jog my memory, that the key words arranged themselves into a kind of a pattern that made me realize how much my own tastes are shaped by what my father was. Because I look down the paper and I have, starting with my earliest recollections in Berkeley, Camping. And when I get to San Diego, I have tennis, and then sailing in San Diego, and walking. Walking is under every place. Different kinds of walks, and at different tempos and with different intents - but always walking. And gathering wild flowers and popping them into the ground somewhere else. Swimming. And it suddenly occurred to me how grateful I should be to the old man for exposing me to so many things which I would say now give me the greatest pleasure in life.

Q: Almost all of them pertained to the out-of-doors.

Miss N.: Indeed. To begin with the camping during the summers when he was teaching at the Naval ROTC in Berkeley, we would pack up in a 1926 Chevrolet sedan - four-door sedan - and take off at the beginning of the summer and make quite long excursions up the coast to, say, Washington and then back again. And this was when I became aware that you could do things the right way and you could do them sloppily. Mother and Daddy had so arranged their camping arrangements that everything that we took with us (and we took quite a bit: a folding table, a tent, hammocks for us to sleep in? -- the car made into a double bed for Mother and Daddy) -- all of the things that - all of the equipment was on the <u>outside</u> of the car, on top or on the sides, or in the front...

Q: Tied?

Miss N.: Tied, and the trunk itself let down into a little instant galley where Mother was able to get supper going within half an hour of the time we made camp anywhere. Because all this stuff was tied on the outside you could only get in and out on one side, isn't that right, Mother?

Mrs. N.: It is.

Miss N.: But still, you know, it was a marvelously efficient arrangement.

Q: Well organized, and certainly a great deal of attention to detail.

Miss N.: Yes, but as I look back on these happy excursions which were such pleasure to us children, I wonder how they could ever have been any pleasure to Mother and Daddy, because my brother and older sister and I had very centrifugal tendencies. My brother wanted to fish, my sister wanted to collect wild flowers, and, as I remember, my inclinations were to build little stone and bark houses for chipmunks which - all of these things, you know, required a different setting and different time schedules and all this. We used to quarrel incessantly and we would start out with the three children in the back seat, my father and mother in front, and some altercation would finally develop into a real fight -- the drawing of blood -- and one child would be brought from the back into the front seat, one parent would sit between the two children in the back seat, and a sort of uneasy, you know, calm would be preserved until we had a chance to get out and sort of work off steam.

Q: But you say you began to see that your freedom of action depended on that forward organization.

Miss N.: Oh, it was magnificent. We could arrive some place late at night, say 8 or 9, after it was dark, and Daddy would put the tent up, and Mother would get supper started, and it just seemed to be, you know, a beautiful, smooth-running operation. And I would like to record one invention of my father's which I think should be passed on to other generations of car campers (not BACK PACKERS.)

Q: Not patented?

Miss N.: No, it's not patented and I warmly recommend it. He took a regular Navy canvas hammock and since he was afraid that we, being unaccustomed to sleeping in hammocks, would topple out at night, or the blankets would fly off, he interleaved blankets like this - three, I think - on each hammock, and laid out the hammock and took a sailmaker's palm and needle, and stitched these blankets around the edge. So, in effect, you had a suspended sleeping bag, and then even if the hammock did turn over and you lay there, still asleep, with your head hanging down until you turned scarlet, you know, and finally woke up just from discomfort, you did not fall out. It was a magnificent device, and although I now consider a hammock an absolutely miserable place to sleep, because your back is in an unnatural curve, I must say I just look back on those...

Q: Well, when you were so much shorter, it didn't have quite the same effect.

Miss N.: It wasn't quite as agonizing, yes. It was just remarkable. Among these outdoor themes, I should note one other sort of indoor theme that runs all the way through, and this again begins in Berkeley. And this is my recollection of being read to aloud. We were always read to, almost every night, and even in the middle of the day, on rainy days, you could prevail upon somebody to read to you, and I very vividly remember...

Q: Who chose the subject - subject matter?

Miss N.: Well, we had favorite books and some, I think, Daddy was more disposed to enjoy reading than others. But he was really quite malleable and would read almost anything to us. One of the things I remember in particular was a re-telling of the Odyssey, the wanderings of Odysseus and the tale of Troy. I think - I'm not sure - was <u>Odysseus</u> Padrick Colum?

Mrs. N.: I think it was.

Miss N.: It was a beautiful, beautiful job, and I can remember him lying on this rather narrow sofa somewhere in Berkeley, hard, absolutely rock hard, and I think at this time it was Ed. Brewer and myself and somebody else of our age. And we would all lie or sit or somehow worm our way on to this sofa at the same time. And he would just read for, you know, long spells...

Q: He must have read well, then, to hold...

Miss N.: He read very well. He had a, I would say, deliberately low voice, modulated voice, not like any of his children, who tend to be rather raucous. His was very...

Mrs. N.: Like Mary's.

Miss N.: ...unraised, let's put it that way, and he read very distinctly and occasionally just sort of sketching in a little bit of the event, but by and large, he read straight. The way AUDEN reads poetry, you know, fairly straightforward. And, then, to follow this reading aloud on down through the other periods - later periods - of time...I always remember him against a background of bookshelves in Washington and Berkeley, wherever the family lived. His office or study or desk or whatever was always lined with books. He was very easy to buy birthday and Christmas presents for on this account because you could always rely upon his enjoying books

- and it was quite a wide range, I'd say mostly in the field of history...

Q: Political science?

Miss N.: Military recollections, that sort of thing. There are also a few novels which he was fond of, one of which he introduced us all to, a rather - it's now a sort of a classic of the thriller variety, called the Riddle of the Sands... Have you, by any chance, heard of that?

Q: Never. Is it something like the John Buchan series?

Miss N.: Well, you've got the time period right. This chap was an Englishman and the book was written sometime in the early twentieth century, before World War I. It's a small book and a delight. It is an account of a trip in the waters off North Germany made by a couple of young Englishmen in a small boat, and it involved learning about German plans actually to mount a cross-Channel invasion, and the technique of doing so. And this, of course, was long before the notion of amphibious warfare was given very much thought, and apparently this had struck - I think the old man probably read it when it first came out, and he recollected it and he recommended it to us, and now it has come out again in...

Q: Who was the author?

Miss N.: I think it's Childers, but I'm not sure. You have a copy of it, Mother.

Q: This is the sort of thing that the English have done so well.

Miss N.: Yes, and it was full of charts, actual charts, you know, of the area, because it was vital to the understanding of the theme of the novel that you realize what the coastline looked like there, these long estuaries going up into the hinterland, so to speak, where, you know, supplies and so forth could be conveyed by land, placed on board by

Mrs. N.: Erskine Childers.

Miss N.: Erskine Childres, yes. The Riddle of the Sands. I warmly recommend it, Mr. Mason, if you have never...

Q: 1967. I shall get a copy.

Miss N.: And besides being, I would say, a constant reader he was also a rather - he had a very nice ear for writing, I think, if I can - er, that's a sort of contradiction in terms - to have an ear for writing...

Q: Not necessarily. There's a cadence to writing...

Miss N.: Well, he was a rather terse, but rather graceful writer himself, I think, and I think his approach to this was partly one of courtesy -- that he'd not waste people's time by beating around the bush: you are as concise and explicit and direct as possible. And I was amused that when Mr. Potter's chapters started arriving at Berkeley and Daddy was reading them, he construed his responsibilities to include stylistic revisions as well as digging deeper into problems of interpretation and facts. I remember coming into his office one morning and he was showing me the manuscript. I think this was one of the exercises that gave him more pleasure after he left Washington than almost anything else. I think he enjoyed being regent quite a bit, but I think there was - I can't think of anything else,

Mother, can you, that gave him more pleasure than receiving the chapters of this voluminous book in typescript and going through them. And I looked at his penciled notations, and there would be many places where he had crossed out a line or two, and by altering the structure of a sentence had made, you know, ten words unnecessary, and it gave him pleasure to do so.

Q: Actually, isn't it the hallmark of good writing, anyway, to be brief and use the well-chosen words?

Miss N.: His interest in language was, I think, probably most manifest to outsiders in his delight in stories. Now, many of them are stories that can be told ineptly and they still retain some flavor, but there was one story that I remember we all heard over and over again, and it became a sort of a performance. You know, because you've heard the Kreutzer Sonata once, you don't mind hearing it again if it's going to be done different ways by different people. My brother and I in particular were just fascinated by this story and I remember when my brother was teaching at the University back after the war, and Daddy and Mother were living in Berkeley, my father was telling this story to some dinner party, and my brother and I stood at the door of the living room listening to him, and my brother's face was just full of expectation - just delighted - and you could see that my father had worked over this story carefully, and he had experimented a little, altering one word here and one word there, and it had become a real masterpiece. And when he finished, my brother looked at me and said, "God, I love to hear him tell that story."

Q: Tell it to me now, will you?

Miss N.: Oh! It was a story about a young man after World War II, who wished to take advantage of the GI Bill provisions for obtaining a subsidized education. And he went to his VA adviser and said that he would like to be a midwife, And the adviser said, "No, I think you're a little confused. Women are midwives, not men." And this young man -- I guess he'd been a hospital corpsman -- said, "Don't be ridiculous. At every level of the medical profession there are both men and women, there are women doctors and male nurses, I don't see why I can't be a midwife." So, the Veterans' Administration man said, "Well, come back next Tuesday. I'll find out." And next Tuesday, the man returned and the VA fellow said, "Well, it turns out there are schools of midwifery and they will admit a man. I was rather surprised myself." So this man went away to school as he so desired, and he was graduated finally, hung out his shingle, and equipped himself with shiny little black bag full of tools, and sat down to wait for a client. One night, late, there was a frantic banging on the door and a farmer who had seen the sign outside came in and said, "I want to see the midwife." The young man said, "I'm the midwife," and the farmer said, "Incredible," but he said that matters were very difficult at his house and he wasn't going to argue with somebody who said he was a midwife, would he come along, and he did. He went out to the farm, and he had been taught in school, not only the techniques of midwifery, but the techniques of practical psychology, and one of these was that you set your client's mind at rest. So, as he was going into the bedroom, he said to the farmer, "Now, you just don't worry. Everything will be fine. Go and sit down, and just leave everything to me." Then he went into the wife's bedroom and he shut the door, and the farmer paced around somewhat nervously, and the door opened a crack, and the young man leaned out and said, "Excuse me, do you have a screwdriver?" The farmer, with some qualms, not venturing to question this professional, said, "Oh, yes," and he raced out to the garage and brought in a screwdriver. The young man accepted it through the crack in the door and said, "Thank you, very much." The door shut, and the farmer, who had been trying to get a peek inside, sat down again. A moment later - oh, ten minutes later - the door opened another crack and the young midwife said, "Tell me, do you have a putty knife - something with a thin blade, a limber blade?" The farmer, feeling even more ill at ease, said, yes, he did, and he fetched a putty knife, which was passed through the crack in the door and the young man shut the door again. A long time went by and the farmer was at this point beginning to feel great anxiety. The door opened again and the young man said, "Do you have an instrument with a sort of a hook on the end?" And the farmer - his heart just, you know, like this - said, "Well, I suppose I could bend a coat hanger so that it had a hook on the end. Would that do? "That would do fine. You just get that." So the farmer went and got the coathanger, but he could not restrain himself any longer and he said, "Now, look, all these things - what's going on in there? Are there any complications?" And the young man said, "Complications, are there complications, I can't get my bag open."

Q: .... the suspense........

Miss N.: It was a magnificent story and it was usually preceeded by a quite serious and sincere disquisition on how much more sensible we had been after World War II in what we did for servicemen. World War I veterans had been given a one-time chunk of money, which they had gone through or, in other words, frittered away, whereas in World War II we gave the most precious thing any man could have, which was education. And you know, in this way, you could see the audience being swayed one way or another. First, they sort of (nodding) "yes, yes, that's right," then when the story proceeded you really could see their distinct anxiety, particularly on the faces of the women, as you can imagine. The relief at the denouement -- it was really a very artful story. As I say, he polished it...

Q: Was this his own composition?

Miss N.: I'm not sure - I don't think the story was his own, but I'm sure what he was repeating was just bare bones, and I distinctly remember his going like this when he said, "Remember -- a limber knife," and I'm sure that adjective was one which had occurred to him as conveying exactly what a kind of quivering instrument he had in mind.

Q: He was so adept at story-telling from having told so many. I often wonder about the source of stories. Somebody composes them originally and, I mean, he must have been a composer of stories to have such a wide variety.

Miss N.: Well, it's like being known as a shell-collector, Mr. Mason. Everybody who knows you collect shells will, if they see one, pick it up and give it to you the next time they see you. Many people knew that Daddy enjoyed stories and that those he liked best he would think about and tell as well as he could. So people used to tell him stories all the time. I know that when we wrote letters to him, we always tried, you know, when we were getting to the end of the page, during the war, we would review the week and see if anybody had told us any story that was worth passing on. This was the obvious place to send it.

Well, having established these two main themes, the outdoor and the indoor, I guess I'll just ramble on and mention some of the other...

Q: Well, I think you could talk perhaps more about the outdoor you got involved in because...

Miss N.: Yes. He was a very good tennis player, a good-looking tennis player. Not a foxy player, but beautiful strokes and very steady and he, I think, (Interruption)...There were tennis courts down at the destroyer base in San Diego, and among the people who used to play there all the time was a girl named Mary Greason who, at that time, was a student in San Diego Junior College, I think.

Mrs. N.: Yes, she was.

Miss N.: Her father was a Chief Warrant Officer on the base...

Mrs. N.: Yes. Pay Corps...

Miss N.: Pay Corps, and she was a long, skinny string bean, who eventually became a ranking tennis player in Southern California, amateur - and my father was just delighted when he saw her playing on the tennis court, although she could already beat him at that time. She was still quite rash and unsteady and inclined to force her game beyond what she could do with it, and so he would play with her and, you know, he was the sort of person who would say, "Well, now today we'll work on your back hand," and he would. Everything, every ball that came over the net would be at the back hand. And she would just work away at this. He liked tennis so much that - San Diego, as you know, is quite tennis country - that he once had Eleanor Tennant, a tennis coach, come down to the base and deliver a sort of demonstration lesson for anybody on the base who wanted to come. And there were quite a few bluejackets who played there regularly and they all came and brought their families, and they'd sit around and watch Miss Tennant demonstrate and play a few demonstration games with Mary Greason and so forth. He thoroughly enjoyed tennis. I must say I was not able to beat him until after the war, and I had to bring all sorts of devious things to my aid. I played him after he had - after he was recovering from flu. I played him on a court that he had never played on, down in Wellfleet, and no courts that were rather unkempt, and had little tufts of grass growing out of the center and nets which were only about six inches above the ground in the center, you know, very saggy, full of holes. And I gave him a racket which was shaped sort of like a lacrosse stick. It was an ancient racket that came from a closet upstairs and I don't think he was very impressed with this either.

Q: You were taking advantage of him, weren't you?

Miss N.: I was, and I finally beat him. Two sets. And at this time he was, goodness, he was - he must have been in his late sixties.

Mrs. N.: No, he wasn't.

Miss N.: Wasn't he? When was this?

Mrs. N.: Dad was still in his fifties when he finished the war. This was when he was at the United Nations, '51 - '50 or '51.

Miss N.: Yes.

Mrs. N.: Sixteen years before his death. Well, he must have been about 60, yes.

Miss N.: And at that time he still played a very - although he hadn't played, you know, for quite a few years.

Q: He didn't really play during the war, did he?

Miss N.: He didn't really play during the war and he was playing more or less as a kindness to me - giving me someone to play with. And it was just a lovely game. He was, I think, a model competitor in tennis, in horse shoes, in everything like that. That is, there are some people who are nice to play with because if they see you already have two balls, they hold the third. When they send the ball over to you, when you're serving, it comes exactly to you, it doesn't go five feet away. He was a very - I think just a model of courtesy in any kind of competitive sport.

Q: Did you say that they wouldn't permit him to play tennis during the war because...

Mrs. N.: The doctors thought he would find it too big a strain.

Q: Oh, I see.

Mrs. N.: They didn't want him to put that strain on his heart.

Q: That answers a question that arose the other day because Admiral Redman said that he hadn't played tennis during the war and he didn't know why because he knew he loved to play tennis.

Mrs. N: Well, the doctors didn't want him to. He did pitch horse shoes, and he did a lot of shooting - target shooting, and a great deal of walking, but the doctors asked him to please not play tennis.

Q: I notice also that when he was dealing with younger people in sports and so forth, he always had the teaching aspect in mind somewhere.

Mrs. N.: He did.

Miss N.: Bowling.

Mrs. N.: Yes, bowling.

Miss N.: Horse shoes, in particular. Behind the house in Berkeley, our next door neighbor had very kindly on his own lot, the upper end of his own lot, had a very beautiful horse shoe court built with lights, so that you could play at night. It was sort of a neighborhood court - people used to come down from down the street and pitch, and Daddy was extremely good. On a good day he could lay four ringers on in succession, and he could spot you 15 points and frequently get 21 first. He was always interested in techniques. My brother is like him in this respect. Whenever he meets somebody who does something he doesn't do, he's always wondering, how does it work? What is it like to do that? Daddy was just sort of intuitively and instinctively looking for techniques, and he had seen a good many good horse-shoe pitchers pitch and he pitched the classic way, and he attempted to induce all his - everybody who came down to the court with him to at least try pitching the right way. Well, the right way is a way that seems extraordinarily unnatural to anybody who's throwing horse shoes for the first time. It's a sort of a - it's a maneuver of almost ballet-like precision where the shoe describes one and three-quarter revolutions in air and lands flat like this, so that, even if you don't hit the pin it doesn't bounce, but if you do hit the pin it locks on. He would always attempt to show people how to do this, and if they indicated, you know, that time was too short -- they were not going to try, they were going to pitch their own sloppy way, their own uneconomic way, the way which is natural to throw a horse shoe -- he'd always let them do it, and then he would beat them. Do you remember the game with the Holzmans? When Mother and Daddy were at the United Nations, I was at Cambridge.

A graduate student and his wife and little son came down to Wellfleet. This graduate student, named Frank Holzman, was a magnificant tennis player. He was a natural athlete. (A most unlikely person to be athletic -- he looked just like a miniature Groucho Marx.) But he had never played horseshoes. And Daddy said to him at dinner, "Frank, tomorrow morning, would you like to pitch a game of horseshoes?" Frank said, "Sure, I know I'd love to," and as he told me later he said to his wife, "You know, I've never pitched horseshoes. But even though I've never seen the game, I could pick it up in ten minutes." Then he began to think already, in advance, somewhat pityingly, "Isn't it too bad that I'm going to have to probably beat Admiral Nimitz at horseshoes tomorrow." He went out the next morning and they raked up the little sand pits and Daddy explained to Frank the right way to hold a shoe and Frank started pitching. He came in an hour and a half later and he had been absolutely beaten - something like 21 to 3, 21 to 1, three or four games. And he said to me later, "It was right that I should get my comeuppance, but to be beaten like that by a man who would occasionally and slyly apologize for being off his game." That did it. It was almost more than he could bear.

Q: Horseshoes is a game that not too many people practice and play and know about.

Mrs. N.: That's right. When Ralph Bunche came out, and Ralph Bunche was staying with us, those two became absolutely insufferable if anybody came to call or anthing and they would have to give up pitching horse shoes.

Miss N.: Well, I think Daddy thought it was a form of exercise that almost everybody could engage in. It did not require running. The stooping that *was* required was a very desirable kind of exercise for most of us. It did not require strength to play.

Q: It required precision.

Miss N.: It required precision and control, and it was again a game which offered limitless opportunities for psychological warfare. It is deliberate, you know. In tennis, you can't really between strokes, as it were, press your campaign, but you can do this in horse shoes. The first shoe goes down and your comment on this can either inflame your opponent so that he throws it right down into the pea patch, or make him over-eager, make him over-anxious to do all sorts of things, and although Daddy very rarely resorted to this, it is plain that he relished the tempo of this game because it did permit all the people who were playing to comment upon it, how the game was going, and it was a very friendly chatty sort of an occupation.

Q: Mrs. Nimitz, did you pitch horse shoes, too?

Mrs. N.: Oh, yes, I pitched horse shoes with President Truman. Bess pitched with Chester and I must say that President Truman was no horse-shoe pitcher. I was better than he was. We couldn't manage that pair.

Q: Tell me about the walking.

Miss N.: Oh, well I was just thinking that I jotted down under "Washington" all the walks we took in Rock Creek Park, which is a magnificent place to walk - it used to be, at any rate.

Q: Dangerous place, now.

Miss N.: Dangerous now, I gather, but before the war(this would have been around 1935, 1934, and also just before the war) Mother would take us out to the East-West Highway which crossed Rock Creek Park at the very end, and then we would walk back down. Or , vice versa, we would walk out there and she would come out and pick us up.

Q: Quite a considerable walk.

Miss N.: Quite a considerable walk, and I remember Daddy - long before it was common for American men to wear shorts, Daddy wore Bermuda shorts, and he wore socks that came just below the knees, and either a wool shirt or a knit shirt, and then a rather cruddy looking felt hat with a rather wavy brim, or an old straw hats. And he always carried a walking stick, which, although I don't carry a walking stick myself...I began to appreciate the many reasons why one does, and they have very little to do with its - with using it as a stabilizer device while walking across streams in the few cases where you really need a walking stick. It made a nice noise on the pavement, and it can be used to point out objects, it can be used to part the grass to show a flower or something like that - and, of, yes, it could be used in crookneck fashion like this. It can be used to drag down the branch of a tree to pick off the fruit. This was one of the things that used to embarrass my sister and me very much. Daddy collected mushrooms, among other things, and he frequently carried an old issue of The National Geographic wadded up in his hip pocket and we would be walking, say, in a residential area where people might even be sitting on their front porch, rocking, and if there was an interesting specimen of mushroom on the front lawn, he would go right up on the lawn, pluck it out, and ask them if they were aware of what they had. He was a person whom I think it would be impossible to resent, when doing something which other people might resent. You know, it might be considered a kind of an impertinence to have somebody simply walk right up in your yard and start plucking out the mushrooms. But he always had this disarming smile on his face, and before long they would be saying "what is the issue of the Geographic?" and they would have to get one, too, and he would just have them in the palm of his hand...

Q: What did he do with his collection of mushrooms?

Miss N.: Oh, we ate 'em - puffballs and all sorts of things.

Q: It calls for a fine and discriminating knowledge, doesn't it, to know which is which?

Miss N.: Well, it does. However, in any locality there are two or three things that are unmistakable and which anyone can learn to collect. There are even some in Southern California, which is not a very mushroomy place because it's too dry.

Mrs. N.: Oh, we used to have great beds of mushrooms, we'd

get two or three pounds and they'd bring them home, and we'd cook them in butter...

Q: There's nothing more delicious. I agree with you - but you have to know.

Miss N.: He liked long walks. I mean he was willing to walk any amount, any at the time when he was permitted to walk around the block and I'm sure he would have settled for a walk around the block, but he liked long walks. For instance, this walk from under Massachusetts Avenue bridge out to the East-West Highway would be, I guess, about seven miles, wouldn't it, Mother?

Mrs. N.: Uh-huh.

Miss N.: And...

Q: That's actually out to Silver Spring.

Miss N.: Yes. A little longer perhaps, but he liked even better a walk - a magnificent walk - we took after some spring floods out along the tow path that runs beside the Potomac out to Great Falls. It was from Georgetown, where you let us out, out to Great Falls where you picked us up around 2 or 3 in the afternoon. I think it was about 18 miles.

Q: A beautiful walk.

Miss N.: It was absolutely gorgeous, and it was rather a difficult walk at that time because the tow path itself was all choked with the stuff which the flood had..

Q: Washed up... Marshy.

Miss N.: All over the place. And then there were a couple of times where you were just hopping from rock to rock right along the river. You know, way up towards the Falls...

Q: Portage...

Miss N.: Yes, where you just skip from one rock to another. This was, I think, the recreation which, throughout his life, probably gave him more fun than anything else. And so many people who have introduced themselves as having known Daddy would say, "Oh, yes, we used to go walking," and then they would say where it was. If it was in Honolulu they used to walk out from Mauna Loa, or if it was around San Pedro they used to walk around what is now Palos Verdes. In other words, this was the way I think an awful lot of people got to know him quite well, because he was, you know, a nice discursive walking companion.

Q: He was relaxed.

Miss N.: Yes, very relaxed. In Berkeley, in the late 40's and 50's, he continued to walk all the time in Tilden Park, and I gradually became aware that his philosophy of walking was quite different from mine. There is a dog run there, a place where people in Berkeley with dogs can let them off leashes and they can just run free. It is a circular walk which starts with a very steep climb from the bottom of the park, next to the golf course, up to a ridge which must be, oh, 800 feet higher, I guess. It's a very steep trail up, and I have always felt that he should - I'm a back packer, myself - that you should walk slowly enough so that you never stop, you know, you never _have_ to rest, really, just keep striding along putting one foot before the other.

But I noticed that this hill was not considered a real rugged hill, and *had not* been designed as switchbacks if it had been in the Sierra. The old man would walk vigorously at a good clip for about 100 feet almost straight up and then he would be out of breath and he would pause, but not ostensibly for the purpose of taking a rest. It would be to point out a patch of pine trees where the needles were beginning to dry up that had been infected with the red spider or something like that. He would point this out, and ...

Q: A strategic pause.

Miss N.: Yes. Everybody who took walks with him at this time became aware of this, I know. The Grillers and the Batthas and all the others realized that Daddy never stopped because he was tired. He stopped because he wanted to point something out, but it would be a good idea to spin out the conversation a little bit so that he did get - or that it was his option when he would begin. Then he would forge on.

Q: He made no concessions to age, then?

Miss N.: That's right. Not a bit. He liked to feel that he was not   , that he was still able to walk with, you know, anybody, that he was just as good a walker as ever and, indeed, he was, but the thing is some people start by setting a somewhat more deliberate pace. He wouldn't, he just wouldn't, he was just going to keep up the old tempo and then stop if he had to, but not seeming to rest. Another thing that I recall about these walks besides his shorts and his walking stick and his battered hat, was that a dog was always on these walks. Either a little gold and white cocker - liver and white cocker - no, gold and white, named Freckles (in Washington and the early years in Berkeley) or a little wire-haired, long-haired dachshund named Dina. I think she was the only beast that ever absolutely foiled my father, because she would take off into the underbrush and he would hear her licences jingle and he would stand and wait for her, and she would have found some interesting smell or rustle down in the bushes and she just refused to come out. As long as you called, she was aware that you were there and she would not come out. And it wasn't until he learned the technique of remaining stoney silent that she began to suddenly realize that he might have gone, and then she would come out, and then he would grab her by the scruff of the neck and say, "Dina, if you ever do that again, I'll murder you!" And, finally Gigi was a beautiful big black poodle.

Q: That's the one that lives here?

Miss N.: Yes, that's the one that the Pughs have now. One of the ingratiating characteristics that I think that Daddy had about dogs was that he would always assume that when, you know, something the size of a wolf with teeth three inches long and hair standing up on its back like that come roaring out of a yard, Daddy would say very blandly, "Play with that dog, Gigi, play with that dog." I just dreaded it but there would not be a dog fight. He was almost always justified. I don't know why. I wouldn't know but I go walking with my two dogs - two German shepherds - I'm always wondering when I see a stranger. As a matter of fact my instinct when I see a dog that we haven't encountered before is to assume that I should take steps to prevent somebody beating up somebody else. His conception on the other hand was rather that you established the right mood by saying in this commanding tone, "Play with him," everything would be all right and, by and large, it was. I can't remember him ever being involved in a dog fight, can you?

Mrs. N.: No. But it always used to tickle me so. It was certainly an example of, you know, a really tranquil assurance that there was nothing that you couldn't handle with a dog.

Q: He always liked to have a dog around, then?

Miss N.: Oh, yes. Actually...

Q: Did he have a wartime dog?

Miss N.: Yes, Makalopa, a Schnauzer.

Mrs. N.: During the war, he had a Schnauzer...

Q: This was in Hawaii?

Mrs. N.: Guam.

Miss N.: Was it Guam.

Mrs. N.: I think it was Guam.

Miss N.: Oh, yes. I think that's another thing that he passed on to all his children besides a love for walking, and that is the notion that you have a dog - people have dogs - or vice versa. But at any rate, there is not such a thing as not having a dog. It's not that you even consider the alternative. You have a dog. In fact, I think that he would have relished, you know, the sort of appreciation of dogs revealed in the Schultz Snoopy Cartoons. You know the one last week of Charlie Brown saying to Snoopy, "Snoopy, there's going to be a dog show tomorrow." And then in the next frame, he says, "Snoopy, have you ever thought of entering a dog show?" And in the third frame, Snoopy by himself is saying, "What a ridiculous idea." Then in the final frame he says, "I don't even have a dog."

Mrs. N.: Well, we might say that Makalapa, the dog that the Admiral had during the war, the Admiral liked it and the two mess boys liked the dog, but everybody else on the Island hated it because it had taken a piece out of practically everybody. It didn't like people. As the aide said, "There are more people who'd like to kick the dog under the table." But he did not bring the dog back; he gave it to someone, because our Freckles was still alive and he wouldn't bring that dog back to the family.

Q: But he had to have a dog as a companion.

Mrs. N.: Well, somebody gave him this dog. Actually, I don't think the dog was much comfort to him, because he wasn't a fun dog the way that our other dogs were; he was overbred.

Miss N.: I gather he was not a very demonstrative or friendly animal.

Mrs. N.: No, he'd go to sleep under Chester's desk all day long.

Miss N.: Another thing about a dog is they're telling you how nice things are, and...

Q: They're so flattering, aren't they?

Miss N.: Yes, and how well you look this morning - this sort of thing. I gather this was not that kind of a dog. He served one function only, which is to go for walks. Well, I reckon that's not a contemptible function. If a dog can go for walks, that's something. Thinking of dogs and what I remember of Daddy's characteristic utterance - mode of utterance, which is the unraised voice...I remember when he was in Topanga and I had a young dog (a German shepherd, collie, and heaven only knows what else, a mixture, who was about perhaps nine months - ten months - at that time) and at the breakfast table, my father said, "Have you taught this dog how to speak?" And I said, "No." So he said, "Well, I think she should learn." And with a fragment of bun or something, he said, "Speak, Kate, speak!" and she listened very intently and finally - I was amazed, she did say, "Woof." And he said, "Louder." He said very softly, "Louder," and I don't know how she got the idea, but she began to bark a little more loudly, and he was very pleased. Remember, he had Dina rolling over. Did you teach her that?

Mrs. N.: No, I think he taught her.

Miss N.: But he was speaking so softly, "Louder, Kate, louder". It was such a delicious contradiction.

Q: What about his swimming prowess?

Miss N.: Oh, he was a very strong swimmer and absolutely impervious to cold, as far as I was concerned. I remember one October, during a Cape Cod Indian summer when he was at the United Nations, he came down to Wellfleet for a weekend and we went for a walk out through the woods - just a gorgeous walk, out in the pine woods. We passed a whole lot of ponds and out to Back Shore, which is the Atlantic. In July that water is, to my mind, almost uninhabitable, and in October (even though the day is nice and there is a little sort of disc of sunshine between your shoulder blades as you walk along the road) it is <u>freezing</u>. And he got out there, and it was so funny -- he was wearing his shorts, as usual, and he peeled them off and it turned out that he had bathing trunks underneath them, and while I - I just didn't want to look, you know - he walked down on the beach and got into the surf, swam out beyond the surf, and swam back and forth, I would guess, oh, about a quarter of a mile in all - he must have been in the water for, oh, I don't know, fifteen to twenty minutes, and then came out. And as he was out there, an elderly trio got out of the car and sat down on the beach, and they saw him and they were just, you know, they were just flabbergasted. And as he came in and dried himself in very leisurely fashion, they struck up a conversation, because they just simply didn't believe that anybody would go in the water at that temperature and at that time of year, let alone a man who seemed to be - well - pretty well along in years, and it turned out that they were of German origin and the man, the old man who was with them, had once worked at Blöm and Voss...

Mrs. N.: Oh, yes, in the machine shop, at the machine yard

where Daddy had studied...

Q: Diesel engines?

Miss N.: Yes, diesel engines, for a while before the war. Well, they had a fine talk about Blöhm and Voss and he came back. And another time, he went swimming out in the Pacific - a ranch out near Tåmales Bay. And this was, although it was in June, you may be aware that the water up here is also very cold - and I went in out of pride - and also it was a very hot day - but I stayed in for about one minute and I came out and it seemed to me that the marrow of my bones was blue all afternoon. I lay on hot sands and there was this little core of cold, you know, running down every arm and leg, and Daddy stayed in again for about a half an hour, swimming back and forth and back and forth, and it didn't seem to bother him.

Mrs. N.: But for the last few years, he didn't go swimming at all. I mean, he'd go in for just a second and come right out.

Miss N.: Yes. He had, I think, a contempt for pools...

Mrs. N. Very definitely.

Miss N.: He liked natural water, either the pond at the Cape, or the bay or the ocean, but he liked real water and...

Q: I suppose in the final days he was beginning to feel the cold.

Mrs N.: Yes, and I think that he had enough aches and pains so that swimming for a long time he did feel the cold and not be comfortable, because he would only stay in for a very short stretch, and then he'd come out and get dressed or lie on the sand, rather.. He loved sun. . He took too much sun, actually, they had to stop him. He could stay out in the sun. He'd go out there and sleep for two hours right in the sun. It always worried me very much. I finally did get him to put a hat on, but he loved to take his sun bath. Miss N.: Yes, he thought everyone should take a sun bath. I remember another of the admonitions that we used to get while going for walks with him was - yah, he'd peel his shirt off, the minute he got out of civilization, he'd take his shirt off and walk in an undershirt so he could get as much sun as possible - and he would say to my older sister and me, "Why don't you take your blouse off. Take your sweater off. Get some of the sun." And we'd say, "It ain't quite the same, you know, If people should suddenly come upon us, how you would like to be seen walking down the path with a couple of half-naked women?" And he could never understand why we'd even consider this trivial matter. Now I think he was - not impervious to the casual opinion of others - but he really esteemed it properly. In other words, you just don't really pay too much attention to what people who don't matter Toyas may think of you. You know, you do pretty much as you like. One recollection dating from San Diego that has always stuck in my mind because it conveyed a great lesson to me - which is that you can convey a great annoyance, even fury, without raising your voice. Somebody had brought me a Filipine dagger, a sort of a   dagger, with a very heavy blade and light handle. It would occur to anybody to throw it, and it occurred to me. We were living on the Regel at that time, steel decks, steel bulkheads, very few places to throw a knife. Now, of course, I should have gone ashore and pitched it at an old barrel somewhere out on the beach, but that did not occur to me. I looked around for the one wooden bulkhead there aboard, and this was a little box housing a refrigerator right outside the galley, and I practised knife-throwing against it, and I was - I could stick it in quite well. Anyone could stick it in. It was a knife that was made for throwing. And one day, the day before there was to be an admiral's inspection...

Mrs. N.: The day of the admiral's inspection...

Miss N.: Oh, the day of the admiral's inspection?

Mrs. N.: Yes, they asked about it.

Miss N.: Daddy was walking around in advance - just to sort of take a quick look around - and he saw this ice box covered with, you know, with punctures and he said, "Who did that?" and he was told that I had done that.

Mrs. N.: He was not told. The boys, all of them, said "We don't know" because they adored Nancy and they weren't going to tell on her. And none of the sailors would tell how it happened. He came in to lunch and he said to me, "I'm going to find out who did that." And I said, "Well, just wait. Don't ask any more of the sailors or the boys. When your daughter comes home, may be she can tell you."

Miss N.: Well, he said, "Come with me," and we went out and I had a sinking feeling as we were approaching the ice box, and there was this wall just riddled, and he said, "Did you do that?" And I said, "Yes." And he said, "Do you think that was very smart?" And I was just quaking in my boots, and I said, "No." He walked away. As he walked away, I had never been quite so aware of -- you know, it was much better than a tirade. It conveyed really almost contempt - how could anybody be so stupid, how could my own child be so stupid? I'm sure that he must have realized early on - I think probably he was a man of natively rather, rather violent tendencies, and I think probably he deliberately refrained from raising his voice most of his life because he realized that if you allow yourself to act angry, then somehow it wells up. It's the old, you know "he runs - you're afraid because you run; you don't run because you're afraid." And I think this instinct in him was very firm, but if he had ever permitted himself to rant and rave that he probably could have broken somebody's head, don't you think so?

Mrs. N.: Yes.

Miss N.: And it was the fact that he deliberately kept his voice down and deliberately used always polite words, you know, he never swore. I never heard him swear in his life. The one thing I can remember him saying on occasions of frustration was, "Gosh all hemlock." And when <u>Mr. Roberts</u> and other books about World War II came out, he simply could not believe that people spoke that way, and we were incredulous, you know, we children. We said, "Daddy, they do."

Q: This is the way it is.

Miss N.: This is the way it is, and I think he must have known the way it is, but he just didn't like to use that sort of language. Again, I think, partly out of fastidiousness and...

Mrs. N.: He wouldn't let the he'd say, "Jesus Christ." and as he frequently did when we were first married. He would say, "I'll help you wash the dishes," and then he would take one of my beautiful cups and instead of filling a dishpan or anything, he would hold it under the hot-water faucet, and this would be in an apartment where the water was boiling hot, and he would drop the cup and break the cup, and his only comment was "Jesus" which was typical because he came from a Mexican area, you know, where this was constantly used. He'd look at me then and say very blandly, "Well, after all you wouldn't want any germs on the cup. It had better be broken than have germs on it."

Miss N.: Oh, yes, he could, I think, brazen it out.

Mrs. N.: Yes, he could.

Miss N.: With more aplomb than anybody. He knew perfectly well that you knew that when he said "you wouldn't want germs on it" that you were just, you know...

Q: That that really wasn't related to the fact.

Miss N.: That's probably another trait that he passed on to her or me, an absolute reluctance to fill a dishpan with water, and also a mad desire to get the dishes done as soon as possible. Chet and I both, I know Joan complains of

Chet, he will practically between courses wash the dishes - the company can hear the water going and, by the time dessert is over, everything is in the cupboard. And I never saw Daddy with a dishpan - always, just always, and he was always saying, "Now let's just get these done." That's one of his utterances I can remember. "Let's just get these done," and then whizz, whizz, and bang, everything goes back in the cupboard. In other words, don't make a big thing out of a trivial task like this - let's just get it out of the way.

Q: Tell me about his less strenuous sports, like cribbage.

Miss N.: Oh, cribbage is another game...

Q: We are getting him indoors for this?

Miss N.: Yes...another game where, I won't say that psychological warfare entered in, but the chance for exchanges, veiled threats or barely concealed triumph, and so forth where there's a lot of opportunity for this. He, I think, perfected the technique, (and this was something else he evolved) of saying before he even picked up his crib, "now in the crib..." as if to say, you know, "the 24, the 20, I have in my hand is just nothing. I'm just going to <u>pulverize</u> you with what I have in my crib." And he always used to say this with great confidence, and you only remember the times when it works, you know, and not the times when it doesn't, and he was a very good cribbage player. He and Mother are both extremely good cribbage players. They are not the compulsive type who do, in cribbage, the equivalent of drawing to an inside straight in poker, you know. They really played the odds, and they played the game almost as though the odds were instinctive, and I don't think that any...

Mrs. N.: Up to within a month or two of the time he died, he and I played cribbage always from 5 to 6 in the afternoon. He would sit there and the mess boy would bring us in a cocktail and when our granddaughter was with us, she was taking some courses at Cal, she would join us. While we played cribbage she would do the crossword puzzle, occasionally asking what was something we'd be doing or the answer to some problem on the puzzle. And I look back on those as very delightful times.

Miss N.: I never played poker with the old man.

Mrs. N.: Oh, he was wonderful at playing poker, and he loved it so. He would not, under any conditions, play bridge.

Q: He didn't play bridge?

Mrs. N.: No, because he said it was always - your partner was likely to get angry at you and everybody was apt to get crabby, and he said that isn't so in poker, and he always played for very low stakes, so that nobody was hurt. But we used to have poker parties in Washington and not so many out here. We used to have them in San Diego, a whole lot of them. We used to go over to people's houses and play poker, because we didn't play it on the ship at all because of the example, but we used to have lots of friends where we would go, and I think if one won a dollar or fifty cents, or something, because we would make the stakes sound very big and then we would divide it by ten so that it was pennies, really. But great fun. He loved that game, just dearly loved it. He liked anything where he could use his great charm, and he would bet away and bet away and you had a feeling he didn't have a darned thing in his hand, but he just thought he could stick people out. I think that he really loved that. He would never play bridge at all.

Q: He had to be something of a poker player during the early stages of the war, didn't he?

Mrs. N.: Yes, he definitely did have to be a poker player, and I think that this is - there are so many things that worked towards his being a good commander-in-chief because he was good at keeping absolutely poker-faced when he had to face threats at the beginning, when he couldn't tell them anything, and he quickly learned a Hawaiian expression which he would use to them, which meant, "Just wait a while, wait a while," and that was all he could say. Then, when things began going better, he got a little bit pleasanter with public relations, but up to that point he wanted no part of the press around him.

Miss N.: I think it shows great realism on his part. He did, I think, sympathize with the fact that everybody had a job of some kind, and that the repulsive task of newspaper reporters is to get news out of you that you don't want to give them. And I think it showed great instinct, I don't think it was conscious, but I think showed great instinct on his part to have learned that Hawaiian phrase - you know like something colorful you can stick in a story - it enables you to say something about a man even though you can't say anything about the war.

Q: Something for the reader to focus on even though he doesn't say anything.

Miss N.: Exactly. Exactly, but it showed, I think a great gift...and I don't think this was really too conscious - for putting himself in somebody else's position, and providing something which, you know, would kind of fill the gap in hard news.

Q: When there was nothing he could say.

Mrs. N.: Go on talking

Miss N.: Well, let's see. Oh, another instructive incident which has remained in my mind - I was a very idiotic would-be young Communist in my late days at George Washington University...

Q: That was, when, in the..?

Miss N.: Right before the war. In 1939 and 1940.

Q: There were many opportunities in Washington in those days.

Miss N.: Oh, yes.

Q: I know from personal experience.

Miss N.: Indeed. Well, I remember one of the humiliations of my life was that I did apply for membership - all the friends I had, or many of them, were members of the YCL at that time, and I was really a very undedicated radical - a very literary sort of radical - and I did ask them idly one day, how do you join? And they said, well, you know, you are considered, your entrance is weighted, it's not a trivial step to take. And I said, "Well, find out if I could be one," in a sort of idle way, and Norman Rose came back later and said, "They said no." I said, "Why not?", because I considered myself a very articulate spokesman for the cause even though I really didn't devote any time to it, and they said, "Because you have a bourgeois background." I felt, "Oh, no! Underprivileged child! I have a bourgeois background." At any rate, during this, I'm sure very difficult phase for everybody, not difficult because I....

Q: You didn't conceal your convictions at home?

Miss N.: No, not at all, and I think it hurt them in - I know that it must have been aggravating for both you and the old man, just to think that somebody could be so stupid, so unanalytical, so unobjective. Not that you embraced a cause that was unpopular or perhaps perverse or something, but that you didn't go about it in any sensible way. I remember one conversation one night, right after the Royal Oak had been sunk. I reported at the dinner table that it was rumored that the British had themselves sunk the Royal Oak in order to, you know, enlist more sympathy for the British cause, and my father put his fork down and he looked at me incredulously. I felt glad I'd reported it as a rumor and not something that I believed myself. And he said with real coldness, "People who would believe that would believe anything." He had really - I think suddenly a vista of how stupid people could be, and that did make an impression on me. During the same period, we went down the Potomac in the Secretary's yacht, you remember?

Q: Sequoia?

Miss N.: What was the name of it?

Mrs. N.: I forget right now.

Q: The _Sequoia_?

Miss N.: A big motor yacht of some kind, not a sailing boat.

Mrs. N.: I can't remember.

Q: With the Secretary of the Navy?

Miss N.: Yes, and on the way down the river, we met the President's yacht coming up the river with Roosevelt aboard and, of course, everybody on the _Sequoia_ tumbled out on deck to stand at attention as the President's yacht went by. We had all been in the cabin when the coxswain came down and reported that the President's yacht was passing, so Daddy went up on deck, and I said somewhat churlishly, "I don't know whether I want to salute Roosevelt," and he said, "Up on deck!" as he was going up the ladder up on deck. "Whether or not you salute Roosevelt is your own business, but you are going to salute the President." And this too sank in.

Q: But it sank in, right?

Miss N.: It sank in.

Q: Say something about his other interests, secondary, the wild flowers and shells and things.

Miss N.: Oh, I think one of the things which gave him most pleasure was this walk up in Tilden Park where he tried for three or four years to establish clumps of yellow lupine. Yellow lupine is almost a shrublike plant which flourishes along the coast where it gets fog, and it will survive and get bigger and more beautiful every year where it gets fog, but inland (where it's dry) it doesn't tend to prosper. Well, he loved it and - I don't know - where did he get those yellow lupine seeds?

Mrs. N.: He got them — there was a great deal of it on Yerba Buena Island, so he had someone on Yerba Buena collect about two quarts of these seeds for him, and then the next year he would walk along with his pocket full and he'd take his cane, and he'd drop a seed in, then he'd go on, and it finally grew around what is now Nimitz Way up on the top of the hill.
Miss N.: And it gave him great pleasure when the Battha children came over or whenever I came up from Santa Monica, we would always go for a walk out there and he would say, "now, just touch these, just touch these," and he would point out the lupines, and he knew there was a little pond up there where the water cress was. In general, he was almost like a proprietor, it almost almost like Tilden Park was almost his own estate, he knew it like the back of his hand, and there wasn't a trail there that he had not walked on at one time or another and where if you walked again you couldn't say, "I remember the last time, I remember the so-and-so." He was just attached to practically every point in that park by recollection, and when I finally got a house in Topanga with a little land of my own, he was very interested in what was going to go into it. It had a little orchard attached to it with three almond trees, and there were a couple of old citrus trees around, and he said, "Every house should have a walnut tree, and every house should have a black fig tree," and then he reflected and then he said, "Well, I don't know whether black

figs would do here. You find out what kind of figs grow in Topanga and we will get you a walnut tree and a fig tree." He did want me to get a pecan, too. I was dubious about whether a pecan would grow there, and I rather resisted it at the time. I now have a pecan tree growing which I got from somebody at work - a volunteer - in their back yard - and when they came down the hall saying, "does anyone want a pecan tree?" I thought of Daddy and I said, "yes." So it's about so high, it does very well. I don't know how good a gardener he was, but he certainly - I don't think he even approached you, Mother, in knowing - or in patience to do things carefully, you know, like weeding and all that, but he did just love it. Particularly trees...

Mrs. N.: And have a compost heap...

Miss N.: Yes.

Mrs. N:.. that was one of his choice...

Miss N.: Yes, he had a compost heap in the back - he built a bin for it - a very ingenious one with sliding sides so that you could get the compost out at different stages, you know, and he was always tossing grass and other things into it. Also he enjoyed the sort of engineering part of gardening. I know we had a stone wall which fell down after some rain, wasn't it?

Mrs. N.: Yes.

Miss N.: And it was the whole chunk of wall, and he borrowed from somebody some sort of a jack - something at any rate which multiplied the amount of force that you yourself apply to something like that, and he jacked this wall back up all by himself and he was markedly pleased by that. But I think he was a tree man more than anything else, and the tree that I will always associate with him is that big weeping pine in front of the house. You bought it, but...

Mrs. N.: I didn't buy it.

Miss N.: Didn't you? Given to you was it?

Mrs. N.: He was away, I think, at the time I put it in, but he certainly loved it.

Miss N.: He just loved to see that tree grow, and it was a rewardingly fast grower with long, long silky needles, and...

Mrs. N.: It was the kind of tree that people would stop in front of the house and come in and ask him what kind of a tree it was. And then he'd go over and fondle these needles and tell them what kind of a tree it was, and then they would say, "Can we buy one anywhere?" And after a while the nursery began to put in a few. People seemed to be anxious...

Q: To make inquiries about it.

Mrs. N.: I know he planted one down at San Dominica, I mean at Santa Catalina, and he planted two or three over at the convent.

Miss N.: You know, he would have, I think, deeply relished, and I wish I had though to send this to him, an essay by Orwell - it appears in "Shooting an elephant" - and it's called "A Good Word for the Vicar of Bray." It's a very brife essay and Mr. Orwell tells how, near a place where he once had a cottage, there was a little church that had once been the living of the Vicar of Bray who was apparently a turn coat - with every party, in and out, a man of rather ignoble nature, but he at one time had planted a yew tree, a gigantic thing, a hundred years old by then, which Orwell had never failed to delight in every time he looked at it, and he reflected that the Vicar of Bray was really a rather bad man, but if you weigh him by what he left and consider that tree, that ~~kx~~ you couldn't help being grateful to him. And then he said that this had made him think, and he looked back on the places he had lived in and the places where he had bought a little tree here and put in some roses there, and he said, "I am far from suggesting that you can make up for your every anti-social act by planting a tree, but if you do kind of jot down your sins of omission and commission and the next spring take the trouble to press an acorn into the bank and tamp it down, and if even one in twenty of these seeds grow, you may ultimately wind up as a benefactor." And I thought this was just lovely.

Mrs. N.: Well, this is one thing I will say, that wherever we lived ~~that~~ where we had a house, that place looked better when we left than when we went there. We planted things, and as she said, he loved trees. He made a real effort to beautify whatever place he took.

Q: Was he ever a member of the Sierra Club out here?

Mrs. N.: No. When we came out here to live, he - I don't think he ever thought of it. At that time, he'd given up ideas of camping or anything. He was too tired by that time, and I think the mental strain was such that when he got away he didn't want to be in any club, he wanted to be alone.

Miss N.: Well, when he first came out here, he was a very morose man. I had the feeling that he thought there was very little worth doing that was now available to him to do.

Q: You mean that he had done the ultimate and...?

Miss N.: Well, it's as simple as this: getting up in the morning and looking at the prospect of the day and finding nothing that was sufficiently challenging or sufficiently rewarding to make it seem like a very appetizing day. He was very morose for a while, and the thing is that his technique of not allowing himself to behave in an impassioned or angry way (because he knew or he sensed - this is only my interpretation - but he sensed that it gets you worse). It's fine if it keeps you from getting angry, but a person of that temperament cannot very readily act as though he were happy when he was not. And you know -- in other words, he had a technique for dealing with rage, he did not have a technique for dealing with tedium or despair or anything like that. And he was just a monstrously unhappy man.

Q: Well, it was new to him.

Miss N.: Yes, it was new and...

Mrs. N.: That was when he took to the United Nations.

Miss N.: Yes, and that, I think, was just a godsend. He enjoyed it, and he was learning something new all the time, and this was something that just excited him. He was meeting people who had experiences entirely different from his and who commanded his respect, and this was a delight to him, and he just sprang back...

Mrs. N.: It was tough on the rest of the family because everybody had come out to the West Coast to be with us. Nancy'd come out, Chester'd come out, Mary was out here at school, and we'd only owned the house nine months, and this was where he wanted to spend the rest of his life, when he up and goes to the United Nations.

Miss N.: Oh, but it was wonderful.

Mrs. N.: It was. It was the one thing that, I think, saved his reason at that time. He was just - he just didn't know what to do with himself. He could garden a certain amount and he enjoyed the people. He enjoyed the Regents meetings, but they only came once a month.

Miss N.: Yes, and the amount of work he brought home in his briefcase from the Regents' meetings would not keep a man of his ability busy more than two days, and, of course, at this time, he was reading. This was the time when books were just coming out on the war and so forth in great numbers, and all these books were sent to him, so he did do - he had a lot of reading to do, and he wrote his own letters, longhand, and he was an extremely punctilious correspondent. If you wrote a letter to him, you got a letter back within two days, and you could almost predict at Christmas and birthdays that the letter thanking you would be there roughly 32 hours after the package had been opened. You could see him looking forward to the day when just to write and thank someone for sending him a book and give your opinion of it and then to look through the minutes of the last subcommittee of the Regents just didn't look like a very deep day.

Mrs. N.: You see, the thing was he had no leave during the war whatsoever and he went right over to the CNO office with no leave, and then when he finally left there, and for the first time since he was a small boy - I mean since he went into the Naval Academy - he suddenly was without something that had to be done by the next day, and this is why I said I gave up the chance to be the head of UNICEF because I knew this was going to happen, and it really did. Everybody had to use a lot of tact.

Miss N.: Most of us must have interests, avocations that are so compelling that we tend to neglect our work for them. I know I do. The old man did not. He was a - he dedicated his life to his work, so that he didn't have...

Q: Everything else was very secondary.

Miss N.: Very secondary, and he did it gracefully and he did it well, but when the time came where he did not have this profession to work at, it was quite devastating.

Q: And when he still had his physical energy. When he had retired, he was...

Mrs. N.: Well, you see, he never retired. He was on the active list to the day he died.

Q: Yes.

Mrs. N.: So, oh, he would be very angry with anyone who spoke of him as retired, and the Secretary of the Navy did ask him once for help and all of this.

Q: Well, by act of Congress, he was on active duty for the rest of his life.

Mrs. N.: Sixty-one years on active duty.

Q: Are you getting weary?

Miss N. No.

Q: Would you talk about his intellectual proclivities and his reading and his meticulousness with grammar and that kind of thing?

Mrs. N.: Well, I think that is one thing about him that I remember with a great deal of pleasure. When we were taking the children camping up at Clear Lake, when they were quite young, and we were at the University of California, the Admiral had just been reading Thackeray's <u>Vanity Fair</u> - yes - <u>Vanity Fair</u>, and he was just intrigued with the characters in <u>Vanity Fair</u> and he would sit there in the afternoons when it was too hot to go fishing, and read <u>Vanity Fair</u> to me with much glee, and he loved the characters. He would laugh over some of the absolutely disreputable characters that were putting it over on other people. But he thought this was a most delightful book. I don't think that he - he always kept by the bed a lot of books that he could pick up and read.

Miss N.: He had another lovely characteristic I think must have given a number of writers pleasure, and that is that when he - if he - read their books and was really impressed with it and really liked it, he would write them a letter. I remember I sent him for his birthday, oh, around 1965 or so, a couple of biographies which, by chance, had come out the same spring, on two sort of representatives of opposing schools in the English Army in the nineteenth century, one the backward-looking type, sort of epaulette, chass army sort of a fellow, and the other the modernizer. Now, I've forgotten who they were, but he wrote to the author of one of them - he was apparently related to some friend of yours here in San Francisco - and...

Mrs. N.: Oh, yes, it was the St. Aubyns... He was a man that lived on the island off the coast of England, St. Michael's Mount.

Miss N.: ...and he wrote him - and wrote him a very nice letter...

Mrs. N.: Lord Lovat.

Q: Lord Lovat?

Mrs. N.: Yes.

Miss N.: And got back - I was so interested in it, the next time I was in his library and was opening his books, he had pasted into the book the letter that the author had written him back, saying how nice it was...

Q: He was the great commando.

Miss N.: ...to hear from people who liked what you wrote. As a matter of fact, the books in his library, many of them, I think he thought of them as not something - he didn't have a sort of a - well, how shall I put it - he didn't have a utilitarian attitude towards books, which I think is a perfectly defensible one. After he had finished a book, he liked to have it by, and if things turned up - newspaper clippings about the author or a letter that somehow had some bearing on either the subject of the book or the author or what not, he would tuck it in, and many of his books had all sorts of things scribbled in - on the end sheets - tucked into them, and he certainly had a respectable library of mainly military history. He liked that. A good deal of Civil War history - which I gather...

Mrs. N.: He was very fond of the Civil War.

Miss N.: I think, Mother, every professional military man finds the Civil War a kind of an enormous lead. Something worth sifting and analyzing and learning from, no matter whether they are - what kind of a soldier they are.

Mrs. N.: All through this book of Yamamoto he's made corrections in one place. He has pencil marks on things that he considered important, and one thing he's got marked, they estimated that they would first establish advance bases in the Marshall Islands, and he put three marks under that. All through this thing... then he has a question mark beside something. They could read the daily reports from Midway, Johnston and Hawaii. It says favorable weather over the ocean was needed for re-fueling by submarines at sea, Although not so successful as the Americans at code-cracking, Japan had succeeded in breaking the American naval weather code. They could read the daily reports, which tickled Chester immensely because by the time the reports reached them, the weather was over.

Miss N.: He not only read an enormous amount, but he had filed away...

Q: A retentive...?

Miss N.: He had a very retentive mind and in conversation titles would occur to him and he would recommend them. I remember a very funny time when a young couple who were friends of mine in Santa Monica and I had done some hiking in the Sierra, and we came to Berkeley at the end of our hike.

And the young man had been a subaltern in the Canadian Army and, at the age of about 18 or 19, had landed on some beach in Europe, and he was fascinated by military history. He'd been in political science at Harvard when I was there, So he was the one who had always told me down in Santa Monica before he met my father, "You know, your father should be writing his memoirs," so I said, "You can tell him that. We've all told him that and none of us have any influence on him. You can tell him that. You can tell him as a man who is as devoted a student of military history as he is that it is his obligation, and that nothing that anybody else writes about him will substitute for the book that he could write himself, which is his own impressions of events as they developed, personalities as he found them, and so forth and so on." Well, Leonard was just dying to meet the old man, and they got along just famously and they were deep in conversation and, finally, Daddy went up to bed around 11.30 or so, and he and Leonard had kept going into his office all the time then coming out again, and it was time for us to go to bed and Leonard appeared with eight books in his arms. He said, "your father says I am to read these before tomorrow morning."

Q: He obviously was a very rapid reader himself, was he?

Mrs. N.: I think he was.

Miss N.: I would say, yes. Probably a much more efficient than ordinary reader. I don't think he approached Kennedy and other people who absorbed a newspaper in five minutes, but he was a very efficient reader.

Q: Did he find, sometimes, in moments of stress, did he find solace in reading? Did he find a relief in reading?

Miss N.: You mean, did he...Yes, I think, for one thing he regarded it, as many people do, as the thing you do when there's nothing else to do. There are some people who will read railway timetables if there's nothing else...

Q: My wife tells me that very often - she's a great reader - and she says that she finds security in reading - this is her security.

Miss N.: You mean that she will go back to a book that she knows because she values it. because...

Q: Yes.

Miss N.: I'm not sure that the old man was that way. The kinds of books that I remember his reading most are not the kind, I think, of book that would offer this kind of refreshment or reinforcement...

Q: Certainly, there is a kind that would not.

Miss N.: He was kind of fond, not of poetry as such, but of individual poems which he would encounter in a magazine or a newspaper, and after he died when we were cleaning out his desk over on the island, we found at the back of the center drawer a poem about an old sailor retired from the sea who, one would think, after all those years of being cold and wet and tempest-tossed, would have relished the snug life ashore and who had expected to do so, but did not, and who remained to the end of his life a sailor still and really quite dissatisfied with life ashore.

Q: Would you say that this spoke a truth to Him?

Miss N.: I would say that his...

Q: Would you read it into the tape, please? But he found something congenial in the idea?

Mrs. N.: Well, it's a perfect poem to fit his situation because it's obviously written in San Francisco.

Miss N.: Was this the one?

Mrs. N.: Yes. This one.

Miss N.: You read it, Mother.

Mrs. N.: It's the "Bluejackets Love and Read Poetry" in Our Navy, Washington.

In Our Navy, Washington, is a queer picture, a sailor paid off and not altogether pleased with the future outlook. It is entitled "Afterwards," by F. A. McHenry:

Well I never go out to the sea again

But tied to a landsman's tether.

I handle a spade, I push a pen,

To keep body and soul together.

Some things I'll miss

The soft sea's kiss

And the tang of gusty weather.

I'll have a bunk that is wide and warm

And a fire where the logs are burning

And perhaps a face in that homelike place

Will keep my heart from turning.

But beyond the pine

The sea will whine

And fill my mind with yearning.

> I'll stay ashore
>
> As the ships go forth
>
> And watch their gray forms crawling [~~flowing~~]
>
> Beneath the bridges
>
> Past the pier
>
> Into the mist that's falling.
>
> And the arms of the sea
>
> Will reach to me
>
> And that same low voice be [~~is~~] calling.

Q: And that introduces another subject which I'd like to ask you. Your brother mentioned it briefly. And that was the Admiral's feeling that he was a Navy man and that having reached the pinnacle and led all these forces, this was the image which he had to maintain to the end, and therefore he could never do what many other officers did - which was - became in the time after the active career, affiliated with business and earned money, because he had a position, he had an image that he felt he owed his people and he had to maintain it.

Miss N.: I think that's quite true. I think that it would have been quite natural for him to have had a hankering to turn his hand to something where he felt he could make a contribution, and...

Q: It certainly would have utilized his time and energy, too, You speak about the void.

Miss N.: Yes, but it would have, I'm sure, been - it might have been congenial in many ways and...

Mrs. N.: I think he felt this way. Bradley went out and took a job to make money. Halsey retired to make money and Halsey did something which got him into a rather difficult situation. He bought some ships or something which didn't increase his stature in any way because it shouldn't have - there was something a little bit off.

Q: Virtually every one of them, wasn't it?

Mrs. N.: Yes, they all went out and did this, and Chester felt that it was important that he, who had been asked to stay on as an elder [chosen] advisor, do it, and nothing was as important to him as to keep his place in history and not mix it with any business, and he knew that I didn't care about money. Therefore, he could do it without feeling that he was depriving me of anything.

Miss N.: That's why the UN job was so wonderful. This was something that he could accept with no reservations...

Mrs. N.: And still stay on the active service.

Miss N.: Yah. He also had, I recall, a feeling that in universities, for instance, he could have quite a - I think he loved his ROTC days here at Berkeley. It was the first time he had ever come in contact with the world of the universities. He found some parts of it rather bizarre because he sat, for instance, on faculty committees that were considering appointments and promotions and this sort of thing, and he was somewhat, I think, bemused when he first realized the publish or perish rule was so rigorously applied, and - er, but he did, I think he was fascinated by universities, and I think all military men are teachers, any professional military man is right if he spends 80 per cent of his time in peacetime teaching, making things, you know, shaping things, which means that they are teaching all the time.

Q: Every aspect of his life was teaching, being a teacher.

Miss N.: Yah, well, he thought...

Q: Dealing with children and with you...

Miss N.: Yes, he thought that, for instance, presidencies of universities should be reserved for professional - for professors - and I think he was, perhaps had reservations about General Eisenhower when he became President of Columbia, feeling that it would have been more reasonable for somebody, a professor to become President.

Q: Did he assume that the professor had the administrative skill?

Miss N.: That, of course, is the great gimmick. I think that with the job of a President of a university having become what it now is, it is a job for somebody who is certainly willing to become a person that a professor is not, even if he started as a professor. But he did, you know, greatly esteem the profession, and I think he sympathized with, although he did not share, some of the sort of, well, some of the things that - the notions of the necessary independence of teachers to teach what they want. And at the time of the oath controversy in Berkeley, when he was a Regent, I think he felt that the issue should never have come up. In the first place, there was no need for an oath to be required of university professors. But in that period when, which was a very bitter one for Berkeley - when Professors who had known each other for years and had some sort of respect for each other, found themselves on opposite sides of the fence, and where all sorts of bitterness and so forth occurred and...

Mrs. N.: He was rather a sort of an antidote for all of this because he tried to explain that if a person was going to be disloyal they would sign the oath without a qualm and go on with their disloyalty. But the people that were going to be loyal would be loyal, that they would get nothing out of this signing of the oath bit, and it was terribly sad at that time because you'd go down and Cvss people, the professors that refused to sign the oath. Their wives would come up to me and they'd say, "Oh...

(Interruption - hot chicken at the door)

Miss N.: Incidentally, I was on a graduate student council at Harvard at that time - and it was a period when most of the professional organizations were warning their graduate students, don't go to Berkeley, and at a meeting of the council where, as usual, we discussed nothing that had anything to do with our business but rather the situation at Berkeley, a young man who had been invited to come and tell about events in Berkeley got up and said to the audience, to the council, "You know, there's even a military man who is not for the oath." He said, "There's a guy there named Admiral Nimitz who's one of the Regents, and even he isn't for the oath." And there was a titter running through the graduate council. I didn't say anything. I just sat there and listened to him saying that even this close-together-between the-eyes naval officer. thought it was An idiotic issue to have raised. He was - he became quite experienced, I think, at the university world and this enabled him later on to be very helpful to a neighbor of ours who lived down the street in Berkeley of Sydney Griller, the first violinist of the Griller Quartet. The Griller Quartet was at one time the quartet in residence at Berkeley, and then Sydney was a member of the Music Department there, and there was apparently a schism between factions in the Music Department, and some sort of rivalry or jealousy. Sydney had been offered the head of the University orchestra, he was to be director of the University orchestra. And in all these matters of sort of worming his way through this environment, which was strange to him - Sydney - he would come to the old man and say, very trustingly, now, what shall I do? Then Daddy would ask him questions and then say, "All right, now, Sydney, you do this." And I always marveled at this - I remember this about three times because they were always in and out of the house, really. One member of the family or the other, either Sydney, or his wife, who couldn't stand the quartet's altercations - she would come down by herself - or his son, who couldn't stand his parents at that moment would come down and seek sympathy, or his daughter who would be   . The whole family was at each other's throats, you know. Just to get away, and they were each one individually very warmly welcomed by Mother and Daddy and allowed to talk until they sort of calmed down, and then they would go on home feeling, you know, just very good again. They were such good neighbors that we had a sort of a minuet that occurred at the end of a dinner if they came to our house. After dinner, Daddy would say, "Now, we'll walk you home" and this was, say, four blocks up the street - it was a pretext for taking a walk - and we would all get out and we would walk the Grillers home, and then when we got to the Grillers' front door, Sydney and Honor were quite likely to say, "Well, now, we'll walk you back." Then they would walk back with us. But Sydney, while inept himself, with this kind of - I won't call it personal maneuvering because that implies some sort of deviousness, it was not that, it was just an ability to cope with a rather difficult personal situation, and Sydney was not a perceptive man in this respect, and he was, I suspect, rather tactless, rather impulsive, and he had got himself into hot water a few times, and then he began to realize why "do this" when I have a good advisor down the street?" It was very pleasant to see them with their heads together conferring over Sydney's next move.

Q: There's a whole area here - maybe you want to exhaust your...

Miss N.: Part. Yes. You carry on, Mr. Mason, and if there's anything I haven't covered, why, I'll be glad to.

Q: Well, this is an area which may be somewhat difficult, but I'm thinking in terms of the biographer and of his difficulties in dealing with a subject like Admiral Nimitz who is so laudatory as a person. I mean you don't hear anything that derogatory about him at all, and yet for a biographer to write a life story and do a whole job, he has to present him as a human being. And so...

Miss N.: If I had to identify the part of his character that strikes me as the most TRAGIC or the, you know, the flaw, it would be one which would not emerge among his - in his normal external relations. It would not emerge to people who had known him in the Navy, I don't think. It would not emerge to people who had known him at the University. But it was this - er, this restless need to have an enterprise worthy of him to do, and an inability to generate it within himself, and a kind of a cold rage at not having something which demanded his effort, and I think in the early Berkeley days, after they came here, after Washington, when he was so at loose ends, that - when he was so gloomy when he would get up in the morning, that I - er, some compulsion would make him attempt to schedule activities which really shouldn't be scheduled if they're going to be any fun, and "Let's drive out to Drake's Bay." All right. "We will leave at 11.05," and this would be sort of, you know, we hadn't decided when we were going to leave, we were just going to go to Drake's Bay. Then it would turn out that he was sitting in the front hall chair with his battered felt hat on and his cane across his knees, feeling extremely irritated because we were all not down there at 11.05, when even the time of departure had not been really firmly established. And then he would be sort of gloomy all the way over and, having a temperament sufficiently like his so that I know that you cannot be jolly when you're in a state like that...

Q: ~~Of course.~~ *You can't force it.*

Miss N.: You cannot, and attempts - anything that indicates that your gloom has been recognized and any attempts to speak to it directly - or even to divert it in too obvious a way - "you see that beautiful patch of wild flowers." or something like that - are just like a red flag to a bull, and make you determined to be more sullen than ever. And he was, he was just - it was just like having a fearful guest in the car, you know. No response, no animation, and I sometimes thought - I used to get, er, it was very easy for me, I could just say "To hell with it. I won't get sucked into anything like this again. I'll just won't take these excursions if he's going to be so sort of unenthusiastic." But then I would think, I have this option, but Mother doesn't have this option. You know, that's rough on her. Couldn't he feign some enjoyment, couldn't he put on? Well, this was *the* one thing he could never do. He could never put on a lightness or a graciousness that he did not feel. Even though it was quite apparent to him that he was making other people miserable, he didn't have whatever it takes - I don't know whether it's - well, I think it's a matter of temperament. He just didn't have it. He couldn't change it, and he did succeed in casting chills over, you know, innumerable occasions. The one thing that would get him out of it invariably would be to have introduced into the situation a foreign ingredient, somebody whom he had not met before, somebody who tacitly expected that he was going to be the kind of man he ought to be, and then he was. But he would not feign -

he could not feign - enjoyment to the family. And, as I say, this is a trait which I think at least two of his children share, and so we have a great sympathy for it, but I must say, though I'm that way myself, it's a very unpleasant way to be.

Mrs. N.: What?

Miss N.: To be churlish and to refuse to put on a reasonably amiable show for somebody who obviously wants you to enjoy it, you know.

Mrs. N.: Oh, I think he did.

Miss N.: Well, I think it was usually - I would say that if I had to put it - now, I think, you know, by itself, this is really very unimportant, but as I say, it shows some kind of a - it really shows what kind of a guy he was, that - and I'm sure he was in a way, not only annoyed, but...

Mrs. N.: It was the result of having been under pressure for so long that he just - he had been in command so long - that it was very hard for him to see something that bored him or something and to have to sit through it. I think he really wanted to be lovely to everyone and to do the right thing, but I think, at times, I don't think to the end of his life, he ever completely unwound, because you can't when you've had to send as many people into battle and not have them come back, when you have children of your own, it can't help but leave a deep mark on you.

Miss N.: Well, I was going to say that the one thing which never failed - where he never failed to make the effort and where he always did it - which showed that he could - was with children, and he could be, you know, he could have spent a very surly day at home, but if he was outside, pottering around the roses or something, and the kids came by on their way home from school and stopped in to chat, he was always patient and, you know, always good-natured. I think maybe it is partly a function of imagination, that he could readily see that you are careful with children, you're polite to children, you're nice with children, and you think of grown-ups as being tougher, they should know how to take things, they shouldn't push you, they should be able to see, but children aren't like that. So when they come up...

Q: It was developed to the point...

Miss N.: ...when they come up and they make a demand on you of some kind, you do respond to it. He did that very well.

Q: But, at the same time, there was a great love for children, wasn't there?

Mrs. N.: Oh, yes, he was devoted to children. I think he really - he loved having young people around.

Q: How do you analyze that particular love for children?

Mrs. N.: Well, I think - he adored his own children, and when they were little, he just loved cuddling them up and having them with him. And I think perhaps his own childhood had been a little lonely childhood, and that for that reason he didn't want his children ever to have that feeling.

Miss N.: I remember he was just an ideal father in the sense that when you came home and said, "Will you take us for a picnic," when he was teaching at the University, you know, he was always good for this, you know, you could always cajole him into taking everybody, driving the car into the park and taking, you know, a batch of children along, and this must have eaten into his time quite a bit, but he was always good for that. I sometimes feel that - we all feel, I think - that our youngest sister, Mary, who at the age when we were saying to him, "Let's go and have a picnic," and he was responding, when she reached that stage, you know, he had no time for this, and that she really got cheated. She didn't see what a patient and amusing guy he could be.

Q: He wasn't physically there, was he?

Miss N.: Right, and on the few occasions when he was back, you know, it was brief visits, just a few days at home, and then when they were in Berkeley after Washington, and Mary was going to Stanford and this was, you know, his worst period. So I'm sure she has a somewhat - a different - can't help having a different impression of him from the rest of us, one which must be much less genial.

Q: Your brother said that when you were small children, you were pretty frisky, as a rule, and so forth, and you got by with a certain amount of this when he was not present, but when he came home, when he'd been on sea duty or something, and he came back, then your mother impressed it upon you that there must be order and there must be less levity than there had been.

Miss N.: One of our camping trips, when the back seat was not separated in time to prevent bloodshed, my brother broke my sister's glasses. This was on the last leg of a long trip home, and it was sort of a straw that broke the camel's back. Most of my acquaintances' fathers would have said irritably, "By God, I'm going to pick up one of you and use you to knock the rest of you down," you know. And Daddy did not say that. He said from the front seat where he was driving, "Chester, when we get home I'm going to spank you." And he drove for another eight hours, wasn't it, Mother? It was a long ride home. And as we drove home, this sort of silence in the whole back of the car, and by the time we got home, even Kate didn't want Chester to be spanked. We all felt, you know, that just riding for eight hours with this hanging over your head - nothing else said, just "Chester, when we get home I'm going to spank you." And when we got home, he was spanked.

Q: You knew all along that this was going to happen.

Miss N.: We knew that it was going to happen and, you know, it was highly unlikely that it could be avoided. It was utterly impossible that he should have forgotten about it, in fact it was not a threat, it was a promise. So he was somewhat...

Mrs. N.: Well, he stood for a lot.

Miss N.: I never did remember, Mother, whether anything happened to me xxxIxmean on the occasion when you and Daddy went calling on Commander Gunther and his wife - this was at the Naval ROTC in Berkeley back in the '20s - and my older brother and I were turned loose in the Gunthers' jungly back garden to play while the grown-ups had tea inside, and my brother at that time had learned that if you pinched the back of somebody's neck like that, you know, they gradually begin to lose consciousness, and he was trying this out on me, and I was resisting. It was just like a scene in the movies where the harassed hero stumbles back like this and feels a brick under his hand, well, I fell back into the leaves and I felt an old rusty licence plate the kind that, you know, the plate, and I hauled off like this and scaled it at my brother and caught him right behind the ear and he bled - oh, how he bled. The most satisfying occasion I can remember and, of course, he raced into the house bleeding and screaming, and the call ended very abruptly before the twenty minutes were up and we were all swept up and hurried home. And I've forgotten, did I have punishment?

Mrs. N.: Yes, you did because you deserved it.

Miss N.: I have very little recollection of being punished. I'm sure we were, but I just - it must have been on occasions when it was so merited.

Mrs. N.: You'll have to admit that they needed it.

Miss N.: I can remember being punished when I threw an electric train - my brother's electric train - out of the window of a second story apartment, with the hope that it would break and it did, and I got a lot of...

Q: Did it hit somebody?

Miss N.: Mother spanked me on that occasion because the old man was not around. I don't remember being spanked too much on other occasions, and I don't remember...

Mrs. N.: At Berkeley when they did something bad, when Chester or Catherine would do something bad, then and Chester would start up the stairs to administer discipline and they'd yell, "Don't you come up. We'd rather have Mother." Then Mother would go up there and administer dicipline, and that would be quieted down, but we early learned that if you punished one of them you had to punish all three because they'd stick together like the rock of Gibraltar. They might have been fighting among themselves in the beginning but they became solid when the parent came into the picture.

Miss N.: Did Chester tell you that when we were all - I remember it mostly when we were all living in Berkeley - I guess that was the last time all of us did live together - Chet was at that time in junior high school, but it was sort of anticipated that he would go to the Naval Academy - I think he wanted to, at that time - and my father had two conversational openers whenever he wished to comment on our conduct and our prospects, and we got so that we recognized them and we would finish the sentence with him simultaneously and that really irked him. One of these openers was, "Haven't you children any respect for your parents," and by the time he got to "parents," we all chimed in, and the other was (and this was addressed not only to Chester, but it was meant to be taken - to be heard and absorbed by Kate and me, too) this was "Now, when you go to the Naval Academy...", and this was followed by some statement of what requirements of discipline and attentiveness and so forth and all the things that one was not when one was not at the Naval Academy, how this was going to change him, all for the better.

Mrs. N.: I remember one night at the destroyer base, when Chester had just come home and -- no, it was just before he went East to school there at the Severn School - and he came in one evening and the executive officer and Chester and I were standing - sitting - up in the upper cabin up in the place where you entertained guests. Chester came up and said, "Daddy, may I take the car?' And his father said, "No, you may not take the car. I don't want you leaving the base tonight." And Chester started all sorts of argument, you know, and I'll never forget the - he said - finally in disgust, young Chester said, "Well, what can I do on the base tonight?" And with absolute calmness, his father looked at him and said, "Well, you know you could read Pendennis."

Miss N.: One wonders whether there was an edge to that.

Mrs. N.: The executive officer nearly fell out of his chair laughing, and Chester just went down the ladder with a feeling "I can't do anything with parents like that."

Q: Your brother spoke also about an extension of your father's attitude in the service towards people who worked for him - an extension of this in terms of his children - and that was almost a silent thing, as I gathered, an expectation, without any question, that you would measure up to a given situation.

Mrs. N.: I think that that was true, that he expected all of his children...

Miss N.: Well, you know, Mother, in a way, he expected everybody in the Navy to do this.

Mrs. N. Yes.

Q: That's why I said an extension of that...

Miss N.: Yes, I remember when I left Cambridge, I was walking around the yard with Professor Gershenkron and (I had been working with him for about a year) I was needing to come out to Rand and I was going to drive out and I had a kind of a rickety car, at that time, and he was saying, you know, I was sort of silly to start off in a car that old. I said, "Oh, no. If there's any difficulty somebody will always turn up." And he said, "What does your father think about your taking off in a car like this?" I said, "Oh, he has always felt that, you know, nothing that - there are no terrible hazards in the world, and he had always told Kate and me, 'If you are ever in any difficulty - of any kind - if the tire is flat and you've lost your money and your ticket, if you don't know where to get any place and you want to know somebody to help you, look around and pick out a bluejacket.'" which is so foreign to the ordinary parent's attitude of...

Q: Protective attitude...

Miss N.: Yes. Well, you know, it shows that he really respected - he really did think that whatever a person might be when they entered the Navy, that the Navy was good for you, and that it could turn anybody into somebody who, in a pinch, would probably turn out more capable than somebody else, and would certainly have more decent instincts...

INDEX

for an interview

with

MISS NANCY NIMITZ

Battha family, 23, 40

Book reading, 4-7, 47-51

Bradley, General Omar, 53-54

Bunche, Ralph, 17

Camping, 2-4

Card games, 34-36

Dogs, 24-27

Greason, Mary, 12-13

Griller, Sydney and family, 23, 57-58

Gunther, Admiral and Mrs. Ernest, 64

Halsey, Admiral William Frederick, 54

Holzman, John, 16-17

Horse shoes, 15-18

Lay, Catherine (Nimitz) 66

The National Geographic, 20

Naval Academy, 66

Nimitz, Catherine, (see Lay) 66

Nimitz, Chester Jr., 33-34, 63-67

NROTC; Berkeley, 2, 54

Our Navy, 52

Redman, Admiral John R., 15

Rigel, 30-32

Rose, Norman, 37

Royal Oak, 38

Sequoia, 38-39

Story telling, 8-12

Swimming, 27-29

Temperament, 59-61

Tennant, Eleanor, 13

Tennis, 12-14

Truman, President and Mrs. Harry, 18

United Nations, 44-45, 54

Walking, 19-25

Interview with Mrs. Chester W. Nimitz and
Miss Nancy Nimitz

By John T. Mason, Jr.

Date: Sunday, 8 June 1969, at their apartment in San Francisco

Q: Miss Nancy, you have something to add to your very interesting comments yesterday.

Miss N.: Well, I think anyone considering my father's mood after the war, when he was living in Berkeley, should probably give a lot of weight to the effect of nuclear weapons on his state of mind...

Q: An interesting point, yes.

Miss N.: I know that he felt that they were non-discriminatory - non-discriminating - weapons, that they could not be pinpointed. He had grave doubts about their military effectiveness in any real sense. I think he was depressed by them. I think he recognized, as most people did, and certainly most military men did, that it wasn't just another new weapon, you know, or something that raises the technological level of warfare by another little step, it was just an entrance into another world. And I think he was depressed by the implications of nuclear weapons. I don't think he was even very happy about good old orthodox high explosives and fire bombings, saturation bombing - Dresden and Japanese cities - and probably had some doubts about that, too. As I recall, he mentioned once the results of a strategic bombing survey which was done after the war on the -

attempting to evaluate the amount of damage that had been done and the effectiveness of the mass raids...

Q: I worked on that.

Miss N.: You did? Well, I think he felt that in the case of Japan, the indications were that probably the blockade had a direct effect upon the Japanese decision to sue for an armistice, and that it was by no means evident that those raids had been the decisive thing. I was interested, a couple of months ago, I was reading The New Scientist, which is an English journal - a sort of a counterpart of Scientific American - one that comes out weekly, and there was a review of a new American book on BW and CW - bacteriological and chemical warfare - and the book, apparently, is by someone who is very much concerned with what the American intentions are with regard to the use of such weapons. You know, we never ratified the Geneva Convention, and the last official pronouncement on American policy was an utterance by President Roosevelt sometime around 1940, I think, in which he said the United States would never be the first to use such weapons. And this book examines testimony before congressional committees and others to infer that there had been a change in policy sometime in the mid-50's, and that it appeared, at any rate, to have been initiated by the Defense Department and it should have been clearly a high-level decision taking in the President and so forth and so on, and he felt, you know, that this was one of the things which should be cleared up, because a decision like that should not be made by the Defense Department. And then he recalled that in an interview with a newspaper reporter sometime in the '50s, the reporter said to Dad, "I guess you had a lot of hard decisions during the war. Tell me one of them." And Daddy said there were a great many, then he reflected, and he said, "I guess one of them was whether" - going in to some island, a very heavily fortified island where there was going to be a very rough time getting in, it was evidently suggested to him that the use of gas or other chemical weapons would make the invasion considerably easier. And he reflected on this and decided that the United States should not be the first nation to violate the Geneva Convention, even if it was not a signatory, and he said "this cost a lot of good Marines." So I think he did, you know, he conceived of his profession as one for gentlemen and I think that may be his being reconciled to Chet's getting out of the Navy later, when he did, was that he felt that in a way the Navy had changed...

Q: Your brother infers this very strongly.

Miss N.: Yes, that all warfare had changed and that, you know, back in the old days - Perry and so forth and so on - a naval officer also was in a real sense a diplomat and made decisions affecting his country's welfare in all sorts of ways that are no longer considered the province of a military man. This, you know, this was something. This was something that really you could apply your energies to and find a real challenge, whereas the post-bomb world is just not that...

Q: It's the age of the specialist, rather than the whole man in terms of the military career.

Miss N.: Yes, and Mother was telling me yesterday another poem that Daddy liked - and it occurs to me that one of the reasons that he liked these short poems, some of which are fairly corny, is that people who write short poems are obliged to be terse, in a way. You cannot ramble in a poem with four quatrains as you could if you sat down to write in prose.

Q: You have to find the exact word, don't you?

Miss N.: Yes. I mean simply the discipline of rhyme and meter forces you to somehow conform, you know, it's an exercise and it usually forces most people, even people whose poetry should never be printed, to be - to pay a little more attention to what they're saying, and they analyze words.

Q: It's a real insight, I would say.

Miss N.: And this poem was one that somebody sent him, some poet who sent it to him because it was about the sea, and the idea is that the sea has not changed. All sorts of other things have changed and you get the impression for the worse, or maybe not for the better, at any rate, but there is something absolutely unchanged about the sea. And it would sort of - I think the reason it appealed so to the old man is not just that it's about the sea, but because it makes the point that here is something which is still uncorrupt - no, uncontaminated -

something that it's going to take an awful lot to spoil.

Q: So, in his mind in his latter days, change was not exactly progress.

Mrs. N.: I know he felt very badly - he knew nothing of the atomic bomb until it went through Honolulu. They didn't tell him. And he always felt very badly over the dropping of that bomb because he said we had Japan beaten already.

Miss N.: Yes. He was very much interested in a series of articles which began to appear - which appeared, let me see, I think it was in Harper's - sometime perhaps around 1955, somewhere in there - about Japanese efforts to negotiate an armistice that started long before we dropped the bomb. These were efforts that were apparently conducted through Russian intermediaries and somehow nothing came of it. Whether the Russians actually did perform the representations they were supposed to perform, you know, or whether - I don't know what it was. But, at any rate, the author of the articles felt quite clearly that Japan was looking for a way to end the war at least five or six months before VJ Day and therefore, had these negotiations gone through, there wouldn't have been this necessity.

Q: Mrs. Nimitz, you say that the Admiral had no knowledge of the development of the atomic bomb. He didn't know about the Manhattan Project?

Mrs. N.: He knew about the Project, undoubtedly, but he did not know...

Miss N.: I would doubt that he even knew about the Project.

Mrs. N.: Really? Perhaps he didn't, I think, because he told me, he said, "I knew nothing of the bomb until it went through my area on the B-20, on the B whatever it was.

Q: B-24, wasn't it?

Mrs. N.: It was a B-24 or something of that sort - picked it up and he said, "I felt very badly about it, because I felt that that was an unnecessary loss of civilian life," because, he said, "We had them beaten. They hadn't enough food, they couldn't do anything. And we also knew that they were trying to get - that they were already trying to get the - somebody to make peace overtures for them, you see.

Q: How did he feel, or did he ever express himself, on the possibility of Russian involvement in the final...

Miss N.: Well, let's see. I remember he was always asking me who had Port Arthur now. He was...

Mrs. N.: I think he felt that the Russians didn't do a darned thing over there, but they wanted to be in it so that they could get their part.

Miss N.: Incidentally, somebody brought me a Russian book on the Russian campaign in the Far East in the last month of the war, and it was called _Final_ and I riffled through the index to see whether they mentioned the old man. Yes, there was one mention - Nimitz - so I looked it up and it was under a picture of the signing of the surrender instrument on the deck of the _Missouri_, and all it said was that after the ceremony was concluded, the American delegation went to Admiral Nimitz' quarters.

Q: Well, that was fair........

Miss N.: And another cause for increasing somberness, I would say, was health. A man who has walked and swum and played tennis and made almost a fetish of being - it was not only that he enjoyed it himself, I think he would have walked and swum and done those things just because he felt you owe it to yourself or to your job or something, to be as healthy as possible. And he was just a magnificently healthy guy. And as his back began to kind of get welded together and, you know...

Q: Did he have an arthritic condition?

Miss N.: Pardon me.

Q: Did he develop an arthritic condition?

Mrs. N.: You see he had been - when he was a young officer at the Navy Yard in New York, a scaffolding fell on him - an enormous scaffolding - and crushed him from all sides. Once they finally - there were some men on this scaffolding so it was terribly heavy, and so when they finally got the scaffolding off of him, he was unconscious. But he came to after a little while, and insisted that he would not go to the hospital, that he was all right, and he was going home. And he came home, and I remember that that night our first child who was very little, two or three months old, Catherine, had a stomach upset and Chester suddenly - the feeling began to come back and he was in agony and he was groaning all night and I thought he was going to die, and I thought Catherine was going to die, and I was all of 21 years old and I assure you I was fit to be tied. I was going just to one and trying to ease Chester's pain, then back to the baby to try and stop her from crying. I think that's a night I'll never forget.

Q: You were growing up fast, weren't you?

Mrs. N.: I was. That is why he had this trouble in his back. The back was injured in that spot and finally it filled with calcium so there was no space for the spinal cord to have any freedom at all.

Miss N.: And this is an extremely painful thing, apparently. When he was over on the island, I know, he would come down to breakfast and be looking quite good, and we would go for a walk down under the bridge and throw sticks for Gigi to catch out in the water or swim out into the water for, and all that, and by the time we walked back he was already beginning to look a little grim, and it was just plain old pain and something that you can't apparently do much for, and I gather that your position does not make you more comfortable - you can't lie down, you can't sit, there isn't much you can do for it.

Q: There's little relief.

Miss N.: That's just it and you learn to live with it...

Mrs. N.: The pain was too deep for anything to touch it, you see. I would say, "Well, now, let me rub your back, let me try to put on something," he'd say, "Darling, it's where you just can't reach it, because there's just nothing that you can do..."

Q: He couldn't reach it either?

Mrs. N.: No.

Miss N.: And you know when you've been healthy most of your

life, you get kind of spoiled, and when you do have something that you can't do anything about, that doesn't go away tomorrow, it's an awful thing to realize.

Q: And pain is not a very pleasant companion.

Miss N.: Yes. I suppose if you've felt fragile all your life, if you've always been knocked down by one cold after another, if you had had allergies and all sorts of problems, you would in a way kind of learn to put up with it, and probably sort of arrange your whole life around this, and somehow learn to come to terms with it, but if you have always - you have managed for the first 65 years of your life to be a very, very healthy specimen, then to have this creeping up on you and realize that there's nothing you can do about it, must be one of the grimest things that you can contemplate, and you'd only be able to forget it for a few hours at a time.

Mrs. N.: You see, that ended by finally, in the last year of his life, here and on the island, it got so bad that he went over to the Naval Hospital and talked to the doctor, and he came home from that visit and he said very quietly, "I'm going out tomorrow and Dr. Clark is going to make some tests, and Dr. Clark asked if you would come." I went out to the hospital and Dr. Gale Clark is - well, I think, almost world-famous neurosurgeon - and he made these tests and I was sitting up in the room at the hospital, and he came up after he had finished the tests and he said that the Admiral was too old for this operation but that the Admiral insisted on it being done, and he said that there was absolutely not a spot of space for the spinal nerve to go through, and no fluid was going through, you see, to make it easy. Nothing. And he said he wanted the operation done, and I said, go ahead and do it.

Q: They removed some of the calcium.

Mrs. N.: Yes. Because you can't let a person go on suffering.

Miss N.: It's a horrible operation. He (Dr. Clark) said when he does it on a junior officer he doesn't send them back to active duty for at least, three months. It's a...

Mrs. N.: And it was one of these things that I felt that the Admiral had given too much of his life to have to live with that pain, that he'd take this chance. And I remember when the operation was through, they called me down and Dr. Clark said that he wanted to keep the Admiral down in the section where he did the operation and also where he would be close to him. So I went in and Chester was practically unconscious in the room, but Chester suddenly came to, and the doctor came out just roaring with laughter. He said, "You know, he came to and he looked up at me and said, 'Surgeon, today I was to have cut the Marines' birthday cake, instead you've been cutting on me.'" The doctor was so pleased because he felt, well, if he'd come out as well as this and still laughing, that things will go well, but the Admiral was always inclined to pneumonia - pneumonia hit him, and he was very sick, and then he began having these small strokes of which he'd had some before. Nothing very serious. One or two were serious, but he did have the satisfaction in the last month or so of not having that ghastly pain.

Miss N.: Yes, because apparently the operation on the spine was just a beautiful job.

Mrs. N.: It was a beautiful job. He cut that nerve absolutely loose so that the spinal fluid could flow again, and he really did. I felt that he was very marvelous because you can't expect a man to do an operation on a person that the chances are against that kind of a thing. Putting his whole reputation on the line.

Miss N.: Yes, Clark was magnificent.

Mrs. N.: And he did this wonderful job on the Admiral, and so - the Clarks are very good friends of mine - he and   .

Q: But other parts of the body were just tired, too.

Mrs. N.: Yes. The situation was that he didn't have that awful pain in his back towards the end. It was pretty ghastly for a number of days. They kept him under a sedative as much as possible, but I guess that was the sort of pain that you couldn't get over right quick. But he did come out of the operation and if only those blasted strokes hadn't started and the pneumonia, he would have been all right. But he did live long enough to learn to walk again, well I mean to forget about his feet and move around. Then we brought him home, and at least he was comfortable for a while before the end. He didn't have that horrible pain, he was in his own home. There was a corpsman there to look out for him and he could have his old-fashioned before dinner, he could play a game of cribbage if he felt well enough - which he seldom did. We had the pleasure of serving his meals, all of them, on this absolutely gorgeous set of china, which the

National Geographic had given to him - cobalt blue edge with gold around the outside, with five gold stars in the middle - and that was quite different from hospital china. At that time, you see, it was the old hospital and the kitchen was about half a mile from where his bed was.

Miss N.: And everything arrived in big steam covered wagons, you know, and I don't think any chef in the world could survive that treatment, and it was very...

Q: Nothing like home, is there?

Mrs. N.: It was wonderful to have him home.

Miss N.: I was remembering last night, Mother, the fact that he was a very sociable man and, at the island, I think it was the year he moved over there, I was there, Kate was there, Niki [Nicky] and her husband were there, and Micky and Peggy were there. Micky and Peggy and Niki [Nicky] were all friends of Kate's and mine that Dad had known for 20 years, since Kate was in college, since I was in college in Washington, he had known these people that long, and I remember we were sitting around the living room, having a drink, and he was sitting in his big chair and he looked out around all these faces, some of whom he hadn't seen for quite a while, and he said very benignly and absolutely incorrectly, "You none of you look a day older."

Mrs. N.: That just made us all laugh.

Miss N.: It was such a nice thing to say and he obviously did feel that we were still very small and...

Mrs. N.: Still needed a little instruction.

Miss N.: But he said it so fondly. All of them, Micky and Niki who had known him the longest.

Mrs. N.: Micky now being the head of the San Francisco Conservatory of Music...

Miss N.: He and his wife are a pair of...

Mrs. N.: Duo pianists.

Miss N.: Not duo, they're one piano.

Mrs. N.: Yes, I guess that's right.

Miss N.: And marvelous, very good. As a matter of fact, I think the same pleasure you get from seeing a good game of tennis or anything that requires dexterity, experience, and skill was the kind of pleasure I got from watching Mother and Daddy function in any kind of a social situation, because they complemented each other so nicely, and I don't think there is a name in the Navy that they could not, between them, remember. It begins with a "-" you know, and then, all of a sudden the other one would get it. This gift of remembering names is not just a gift. It does require some kind of civility, some will to remember or to pay attention when you're being introduced, something which many of us are somewhat deficient in. I spend my time at parties, sort of oozing my way around the table, so that I'm not going to be caught with a man whose name I have forgotten when somebody whose name I do know comes up and I have to introduce them.

Q: You have to slur it over.

Miss N.: Just horrible. But Mother and Daddy never had to do this.

Q: Association is a good gimmick to rely on sometimes.

Miss N. Yes. But I know Chet once commented on this, too. This was another thing like listening to Daddy's old stories, where you have to admire what was just an art - at recalling, at knowing everybody's names the moment they put in an appearance and in recollection being able to evoke names.

Q: How flattering that is, to recognize someone...

Mrs. N.: But what I objected to when I went back to Washington to the CNO house, having been out here for four years, was to see a person who when I left had absolutely bright red hair and when I got back there was with pure white hair. And I finally said to her when I finally recognized who she was, I said, "What in the devil did you do with your red hair?" "Oh," she said, "Catherine, didn't you realize that was dyed. My hair never really was red." And, she said, finally it got to where it wouldn't take the red dye, so she had to bleach it.

Q: This certainly is an added problem today, isn't it?

Mrs. N.: Yes. Oh, terrible.

Q: I was remembering because the change in the color of hair changes the person so much...

Miss N.: Oh, yes, and now that wigs are so common and permit such marvelous changes...

Q: Sometimes you can be excused...

Mrs. N.: Yes, I think so.

Q: In connection with your father's attitude in this period when he was no longer terribly active, can you recall anything when you drove the family West after he left the office of CNO? That long trip, that leisurely trip.

Miss N.: That leisurely trip. At that time, I don't think I was a very easy to get along with person and I was certainly not used to having anybody tell me how to drive. And I remember at one point the old man suggested that I was going a little too fast, which indeed I probably was, whereupon I slowed down and said arrogantly that I had joined the Not-Over-50 Club, and at one point we wished to get some place by 7 o'clock or 8 o'clock in the evening and I was just fiddling along at 50 miles an hour, and the old man suggested that I might go a little faster than that, after all, there was nobody visible for 100 miles. And I remember thinking at that time - I don't suppose I told him the story about the man who went to the pub outside Dublin and he was served a pint of beer which had a mouse in it. He was revolted and summoned the barmaid and she hooked it out with her little finger and left the beer there. And he looked in agony, and she said, "What's the matter?" He said, "Do you expect me to drink this?" And she said, "Huh, he doesn't like it with the little mousey in it, he doesn't like it with the little mousey out of it. How picky can you be?" I'm sure that's a   to Mother, that Daddy and I were probably equally difficult, I imagine.

Mrs. N.: I do remember sitting in the back seat and turning to Freckles once on the way out (Freckles being the cocker spaniel) and saying, "Freckles, I'm glad I'm on the back seat with you."

Q: You were unhappy because you were coming West, were you?

Miss N.: No, I guess I was just - you know everyone has his vanity and one of my many vanities is that I am a very courteous driver and...

Mrs. N.: An excellent driver.

Miss N.: ...and his mild remarks, and it really was only a mild one, just somehow...

Mrs. N.: Well, you'd had an awful stomach ache the day before, I remember that.

Miss N.: ...piqued me enormously and I just...

Mrs. N.: That was a difficult trip.

Miss N.: Indeed, when it comes to being surly, I think I could give the old man cards and spades.

Mrs. N.: I don't think the Admiral was surly. I think he was reserved at times, but when I think of what he went through and what he was trying to unwind from, I think he had a magnificent disposition, because I don't know any one of them that really was as pleasant to everybody, including his family, as Dad was through all of the unwinding process.

Miss N.: Oh, well, the contrast was just enormous. I remember the day he left the Navy Department and left his office, which was on the top deck of the old Navy building, and started down the stairs, everybody came out of their offices and, you know...

Mrs. N.: This was when we were leaving CNO?

Miss N.: Yes. And waved. There were about - I don't know how many - three thousand people all standing by the staircase as he went down. And then he gets into a car and...

Mrs. N.: His wife was with two million men (?)

Miss N.: Yes,...and with his wife and his daughter...

Mrs. N.: I think it was a traumatic experience for him. You see, after all this time and suddenly discover - to realize that he had no one in particular to give orders to and he couldn't help occasionally giving orders to those that were around him. It was a difficult trip and I knew it was going to be a difficult trip. It was the same way I felt when I stood in ~~the Fairmont, and went up~~ to my room in the Fairmont Hotel the night before he was coming in from the islands and we were going to start East, and he was coming back for duty, and I opened the door of the room and didn't put on the light, shut the door, walked over to a window, looked over towards the Claremont Hotel in Berkeley, which ~~was~~ for the first time in many years was lighted up and all, and I said to myself, "Well, the next few years are going to bring lots of problems, but we'll get them all through faithfully." And I stood there for quite a while and thought of the four years that I had been out there working, and of what Chester had gone through and what I knew was going to be a very exasperating time when he got to Washington. There were going to be a lot of things that were going to be very expasperating because he was used to making quick decisions, and I stood there for about half an hour, just realizing that the next morning at 9 o'clock I'd meet him at the plane and we would start on this expedition. You know, I've seen too many of them come home - I knew that this is a terrible pressure that they have to go through, fearful pressure, and that they have to be able to unwind and have to be with somebody that could take the unwinding. They just have to have it.

Q: How fortunate he had you.

Mrs. N.: Well, I don't know. off and on. But I never have felt that our marriage was anything but the most tremendous success, and I've never had him say a disagreeable word to me. He always spoke to me - he might give me a look which would let me know that my value was sinking down a little bit, but we usually ended up laughing over the thing because with the right MIND you can always take over everything. You can manage everything.

Miss N.: Maybe I was particularly unperceptive as a child and never noticed such things as tones of voice and other ways in which you can convey vexation, but I don't remember ever hearing you and Daddy quarrel or even visibly disagree on anything that affected us, and it was quite a revelation to me later on when I realized that people's parents did sometimes explode at each other and throw pots and pans and stomp out of the house, and do all the other impulsive things which one can do when one is mad.

Mrs. N.: Instead of telling their children to read Pendennis.

Q: Cast your mind back to that period at the University of California in the '20s, because you were at home, weren't you?

Miss N.: I was at home. I was...

Mrs. N.: She was too much at home (being sick)

Miss N.: I was not much aware of what was going on, except that I thought the University was a wonderful sort of a big playground - all that green grass and those big trees. One could go down to the place where...

Mrs. N.: Back of the shrubbery.

Miss N.: ...place where the ROTC drilled, and watched them and sort of hang around. One of the things I do recollect from that period. One hears a lot about the impersonality of universities these days, how little contact students have with their - or are apt to have with their professors. I do remember that Mother and Daddy every year, perhaps more than once a year, used to give a great big party for every boy in the unit, and I remember this involved making big casseroles, big chicken...

Mrs. : Chicken noodles...

Miss N.: Big casseroles of chicken noodles and all sorts of things, and that we children were never permitted to come to the party. And we used to hang somewhere on the stairs and look down at all these goodies being laid out, and listen to all the conversations going on and hope that there would be things left over, you know, to make it worth our while the next morning. Did you do that every year?

Mrs. N.: Oh, I'll tell you. One of his first - in the first class of the ROTC and Chester is just crazy about is Arnie Latto (Latout?). He is an admiral who is now retired but is the head of the petroleum and oil situation in the government in Washington.

Q: How do you spell his name?

Mrs. N.: L-a-t-t-u.

Miss N.: He is a Finn.

Mrs. and Miss Nimitz - 20

Mrs. N.: Yes, and his first name is O-n-n-i-e. Very handsome, very nice.

Miss N.: How did he - he wound up as an admiral?

Mrs. N.: Yes. In the Supply Corps.

Q: He's in Washington now?

Mrs. N.: Yes.

Miss N. Yes. You could get in touch with him through them. I'm not sure whether he's in some branch of the government or whether he's with the Oil and Petroleum Institute or something like that.

Mrs. N. I don't know. Anyway, he had charge of the...

Miss N.: Yes, He would be able to tell you a lot about those early days. And he's a charming fellow.

Q: Mrs. Nimitz, you tell me something about that early period. This was a prototype, wasn't it, for the Naval Reserve Training Corps?

Mrs. N.: Yes. This was the start of it. We - our arrival in Berkeley was rather interesting. I had been ill and the doctors would not let me come out with the three children alone, so Chester had had to come back to get me. Well, we didn't have much money, then, and when you had to make that trip East and then come West - five of you on the train ...

Miss N.: With children who ate. You remember dining cars on a train, what the prices on the menu were?

Q: Yes, it was very expensive. Always twice as much as...

Miss N.: And we never wanted those little tiny pots of Boston baked beans. Heavens no, we wanted lamb chops, things that went into money.

Mrs. N.: On the trip out, Chester - we knew we were pretty short for money and I was, at that time, really weak so that I couldn't be around very much. I had to rest a great deal. We finally decided, though, that this was our one chance to take the children to the Grand Canyon. We'd make the side trip. We'd break it and go up and stay all of one night at the hotel.

Miss N.: And we were to go down to the bottom of the canyon on mule-back. This was the big *come-on*.

Mrs. N.: And Chester said, "You know, I've got war bonds from the first world war, and this is what we will use to pay all the expenses." Well, when he got up there he found that he had the envelope but the bonds had long since been used. So we really were upset. The children couldn't go to the bottom of the canyon. And I want to tell you we have some pictures of the maddest expressions...

Miss N.: Oh, we were all *furious*. So they took us for walks around the rim. That was nothing. We didn't want to walk around it. We didn't want to look at Indian sand painting. We didn't want to look at Indian dancing. All we could think was, "They said we could go to the bottom of the canyon on muleback a mule and that was that."

Q: You didn't understand family finances.

Miss N.: Not at all.

Mrs. N.: Well, we finally got to Berkeley and we arrived in Berkeley at about 7 o'clock one morning, and as we got out of the train, there was Commander Gunther waiting for us. He was to be the second-in-command at the ROTC, and he picked us up in his car, and we went up to a restaurant and we had our breakfast. Then we drove up to the house on 1306 Bay View Place that the Admiral had engaged for us before he went East, and he had a delightful conversation with the woman who owned it, and he said she'd leave some of her furniture in it because we didn't own very much furniture at that time. So we could go up there and we knew that the furniture would be there, but to show you the precision with which Chester had arranged things, we got up to the house and as we got up to the house a truck rolled up from the San Diego area bringing what furniture we had, and they started unpacking. In a few minutes the doorbell rang. I went to the door and here was a Captain Fisher in the Construction Corps, who had heard we were coming and had come up to help unpack. So here were Gunther and Captain Fisher unpacking bags and unpacking dishes and everything else, and by night we were just practically completely settled, and the children really loved that duty as well as any duty we ever had.

Miss N.: The house was right next to a playground, Cordinices Playground, and there was a canyon that went down below and it had - there was a huge old live oak tree on a little knoll by the house. It had - I don't know whether it had when we came, but it certainly had when we left - a thick rope tied to some limb and a knot at the end and you could swing way out over this slope and back again. Marvelous. Wonderful place for children.

Q: A certain amount of danger attached to it.

Mrs. N.: I remember one day - she probably wouldn't tell you this - but one day Chester and I came back from some function at the University. I had gotten well after a few months and was able to walk wherever I wanted to, and I - we always walked up from the University and walked around a great deal - and as we came up we saw Nancy and this Eddie Brewer very busy in the back yard with a big wooden crate which was left over from our moving, and they were hammering it - and there seemed to be strange sounds coming out of this crate of weeping. Chester walked back to them and he said, "What have you got there?" There was sort of a dead silence between the two of them. So he said, "Who's in that crate?" "Eddie Aloo." Eddie Aloo being a boy younger than they were whom they absolutely despised, both of them, and he'd been a nuisance all the afternoon, so they just shoved him in this crate and were nailing it up, and your father said, "Well, what are you going to do with it?" They said, "We're going to push him down into the canyon." Well, this was a *steep slope* going down like this, and Chester said, "Unfasten that crate," and they unpacked that crate and the whitest little boy came out of that crate and went like a streak down the street.

Q: Murderous intent!

Miss N.: We really had, and he deserved it.

Mrs. N.: We really had a great deal of fun there at the University. We had so many great friends among the University people, and we went about a great deal, so that I don't know any duty that we had more fun at than the three years that we were at Berkeley.

Miss N.: For one thing, I think it was the first time in his life that the old man had vacations, you know, that came at the same time as our vacations came in the summer, so that we were able to take these camping trips.

Mrs. N.: We went up and camped at Tahoe and Echo Lake for a month and had just the most marvelous time there. I think that was - well, really, all of our duty was pleasant - I don't remember any...

Q: There was no question in that time, as there is today, in connection with the ROTC program...

Mrs. N.: No.

Q: ...of the acceptance of the professor, the naval officer, by the other faculty members.

Mrs. N.: Now, wait a minute. Let's be honest. When they found that this young officer who came here as a commander but was made a captain within about three months, was made a full professor, and here were these grizzled men waiting for their full professorship, there was a little jealousy among some of them. Then when they found - the people at the University discovered - that Chester really had a tremendous knowledge of education and of many things, they put him on the Board for selection of these people and he enjoyed that, he enjoyed seeing what their records were and so forth, and he was terribly interested in it. But when a man named Lerschner, who was quite a famous astronomer, found that

Chester was to teach a course in astronomy, he nearly burst his buttons, and he just came in furious and said - he was the head of the astronomy department, you see - this was astronomy for naval officers, he came and he said, "No one teaches astronomy in this university but people I pick," and Chester said, "Well, now, will you teach this course on astronomy such as they have to have for naval officers?" And he said, yes, he would in his department. And Chester just beamed all over and he said, "This is wonderful, because we in the ROTC are only allowed a certain number of hours of a student's duty, and if it goes over to the University, that gives us so many more hours a week." And this man had discovered that instead of slapping this young man down, he absolutely delighted him. Well, we certainly had three wonderful years there. It was - that was the time when Hoover became President, and Hoover wasn't fond of armed forces, anyhow, and the first thing he did was to cut our pay by 9 per cent, so that we didn't have to - as I said, when Chester made captain, it was the most expensive promotion he had ever had, because we had to have extra stripes on everything and our pay had gone down quite a bit, but we managed to weather it without any difficulty. After Hoover did this, though, I remember when he came up next time - we'd never voted before because moving around all the time he had no reason to do it, and I had not because I hadn't been old enough very long and I'd been married as soon as I was twenty-one, then I didn't have any chance to vote. So we decided we'd register and there was a long conversation between us, and we said, what shall we register as. So we decided that because of my father, who had been a Republican, that we'd register as Republicans, and we voted for Hoover, and what did that devil do? Cut our pay. So we promptly decided, we said, "Next time, it came up we'd register Democrat," which we did. Actually, later on Hoover became a very good friend and...

Q: You found that he had merit?

Mrs. N.: He had merit, and I had known that my brother when he went over on the Lusitania was going to Europe for Hoover as a mining engineer, so I had looked at Hoover - this was why I was so willing to register as a Republican and vote for him because I thought he must be a wonderful man, but he wasn't in Chester's line of business.

Q: Had to be a Quaker.

Miss N.: I would have thought it would be interesting to have been able to talk to some of the professors at the university at that time. I would think they would have been kind of impressed...

Mrs. N.: They were.

Miss N.: ...by the fact that the old man was a reasonable man, and this means not merely rational, lots of people are rational, lots of people are - lots of Dostoevski characters are insane and rational, but he is a reasonable man, and he would be the sort of man it would be nice to have on a committee. A sort of a person whose judgment, I would say, was just awfully good when it was turned loose on any material that it had some familiarity with.

Mrs. N.: Well, I know the man that was - Dean Woods - who was the head of aeronautical science and so forth was very impressed with Dad, and whenever he would go away, have to go away, he'd call Chester and ask him if he'd take his classes. Now Chester didn't know anything about aerodynamics to teach, but this man said "You can give these men a lot that is very necessary for them to learn." And so Chester would take the courses for perhaps a week at a time, and he would lecture to these men.

Q: It's taken for granted that your husband was a most unusual man for an assignment like that, and I suppose you can see that there was a potential for friction with the regular faculty. This seems to be a problem today.

Mrs. N.: This is a thing of which there never was much because Chester was a very agreeable person about making - he was always very thoughtful and courteous to older professors.

Miss N.: Also, he was not a parochial man. I think a lot of naval officers might feel, when catapulted into that environment, "here I am and there are none of us here except me." And I don't think he thought of the University in terms of "we" and "they" but of the University as something...

Mrs. N.: To show you how much of the University he was, years later when he came back as a Regent, he said to one of the Vice Presidents at the University, "Don't you have a school tie?" And this man said, "No," and the Admiral said, "Well, you certainly ought to. What are your official colors?"

And this man said, "Blue and yellow." The Admiral said, "Uhn, there are plenty of blues and yellows. It has to be exact." So, the man said, "I never thought about it." Chester said, "You go and find out what the exact colors are of California, and have it registered what the colors are. Just what..." and he came back and said, yes. So Chester said, "Well, why don't you find someone who will make ties, so that people here with wear their own ties." They did that, and to this day, California has ties - and I was having dinner with this man not so long ago, and he said, "Do you remember when the Admiral brought us to our feet and got the alumni association to put out school ties?" And the Admiral wore a California school tie a great deal of the time when he was out here. So we often laugh over it. Whenever this man's around he says," I shall never forget my astonishment - he said you just can't have it blue and yellow, you've got to have it exactly the right shade of blue and exactly the right shade of yellow." And so they went to the legislature in California here and established a correct shade of blue and yellow.

Miss N.: Very handsome ties. Dark blue with sort of a dusty yellow stripe.

Mrs. N.: No, it was a Yale blue, a bright blue.

Miss N.: Is it a bright blue?

Mrs. N.: Yes, it's a bright blue and yellow, and the ties were a great success.

Q: Shall we talk about the United Nations days now?

Mrs. and Miss Nimitz - 29

Mrs. N.: Let me give you just a little of this, of the start of this. The Admiral and I kept diaries for a while ...

Q: When it was legal.

Mrs. N.: Yes, when it was legal. This one was started Thursday, March 10th, and this is in the Admiral's handwriting.

Q: What year?

Mrs. N.: 1949. "Mostly cloudy and rain all day. Spent all the forenoon and first half of the afternoon in San Francisco at my office and in attending a meeting of the World Affairs Council of Northern California. Called on by Mr. Buckley and one other man, a Vice President of the Anglo-American Bank, an official of the American President Line, and invited to become a director. Was called by long distance by Admiral Denfeld, CNO, and asked if I was interested in being a supervisor - the supervisor - of an election in Kashmir to determine whether this state should go in Pakistan or India. Said I was interested if I could take Mother along. State Department will call me at the office about noon tomorrow. Admiral S. S. Robison arrived in the mid-afternoon to spend several days with us. CW and Joan came for supper." Now, I might add that when he came home from this day in the office, Admiral S. S. Robison was there and he had just arrived and he'd arrived in this rain and I had just given him a highball. When I saw my husband coming up the walk and I went to open the door for him, and as he came through the door he thrust the paper in my hand, and he said, "Don't say anything to Admiral Robison." And he went in to talk to the Admiral, and I opened the paper, and here was this suggestion. You can imagine what it did to me. We'd just bought the house. We hadn't even gotten it fully settled. We had all the children around us for the first time in years, and here he was thinking of going. Well, I didn't say a word but my mind was working a mile a minute. I don't know what I gave them for supper that night, but I did it. Anyway, the next entry is - he and Admiral Robison went to San Francisco and they did, of, a lot of visiting with his friends and so forth, and "during the day I exchanged phone calls with Rear Admiral Woolridge in Washington to get more information on the projected assignment under the UN as plebescite administrator in Kashmir. Also received a phone call from Assistant Secretary of State Rusk on the same subject. I'm to tell Rusk by noon Monday whether I will be available. Mother and I have the matter under consideration." On the 12th of March he says:

"Mother and I have decided to make myself available for the UN job of plebescite administrator of Kashmir, and I will send the State Department a telegram tomorrow. Then I must wait to be chosen by the United Nations Commission on Kashmir."

Then there are one or two days when there wasn't much about this.

Q: May I interrupt to ask how you together resolved this question in the light of your...

Mrs. N.: I really don't think there was much resolving. I

knew what the answer was going to be. It's so much nicer to take it pleasantly. So, Kashmir had been a place that fascinated me because I was a lover of Sir Francis Younghusband's book and had read everything he had written, and so I was terribly anxious to see Kashmir, and we had arranged between ourselves that we would have Mary come out the following year after her freshman year at Stanford - come out to India and join us. So that would be all right. And Chester was going to be in Berkeley for a while longer, so he could - well, we just left the house then, but Nancy was there in the house for several months, and then after that Chester used it for his friends, if there were any of his friends coming through, he would say, "Go out and stay at Mother's," and...

Q: How long a period did you contemplate in India?

Mrs. N.: We had no idea. It might take a year, a year and a half, two years. We had made this decision - he'd made, I'll say he made the decision - and then he had to make a trip down to Hueneme to look over the station there...

Q: To where?

Miss N.: Port Hueneme. It's the naval ordnance test center - no, Port Hueneme is the port next door to the naval ordnance test center. It's just south of Oxnard.

Mrs. N.: We had two or three days there while they were waiting to hear whether he would be accepted. We had lots of fun during that time. We were apparently doing all sort of things. Then comes - I guess it's - yes, this is the next one. He said: "Spent yesterday in the office. Received a phone call from Mr. Cordier, executive assistant to Trygve Lie, United Nations, to say that Pakistan and India had agreed to my nomination as administrator of plebescit in Kashmir. Secretary General Lie asked that I proceed at the earliest possible moment to New York for conference with UN Commission and appropriate officials. Called the Secretary of Navy and asked for a plane for Wednesday night, the 23rd of March, to proceed to Washington, which Sullivan graciously approved. Arranged to stay with the Schifflers in Washington. Busy most of the day making re-arrangements and adjustments." That wasn't half as busy as I was making re-arraggements and adjustments.

Q: That's aside.

Mrs. N. And on the 22nd, "we all went down and had supper with Chester and Joan. Another very busy day packing and so forth. Early in the day I received a telegram from Trygve Lie confirming the fact that I had been accepted for the administrator of the Kashmir plebescite. He asked my early arrival in New York for conference. Had a long telephone conversation with Wooldridge in Washington. We plan to leave from Moffett Field at 6 o'clock tomorrow, which means leaving the house at 4.30. Very busy day making preparations for the departure for Washington. In the office in the forenoon and home by noon. Bruce and Elizabeth Canaega came to see us at 3.40 and at 4 we left the house with cars of baggage for Moffett Field. Took off in an R-5D plane, captain Lieutenant Thomson, an old friend, at 7.30 and after a smooth trip, we landed at the Washington National Airport at 9. Lieutenant Page, Sergeant Cozard and I each had four immunizing shots in the early forenoon (I had taken five shots the day before - the day we left, so I didn't have to have these) and by night we were all very uncomfortable and as was Mother who also had her shots the day before."

We stayed in Washington while he saw the Secretary of the Navy and he saw the Achesons, who was then Secretary of State, and so forth. "I went to the State Department where I remained until 5.30, except for a brief period from 3 p.m. to 4 when I went to the White House to see Admiral Leahy get a third Distinguished Service Medal. During the day I received calls from the Indian diplomatic officials here, also from the Pakistani group. Both pleasant, both assured me that they would do everything to make my plebescite job a success. Had long talks with the State Department people and also with Major General Frank McCoy and with Sarah Wambaugh to receive their ideas. Both have much experience in plebescites."

Q: Who was Sarah Wambaugh?

Mrs. N.: She was the daughter of a professor at Harvard. Her father had written many books on plebescites. She had been one of the tops in the plebescite, as I remember, of Tacna-Arica, which happened years ago, down in the southern part of the country - in South America, and she was a very pleasant lady, but with great knowledge of plebescites.

Q: That was between Chili and Bolivia, wasn't it?

Mrs. and Miss Nimitz - 34

Mrs. N.: Yes. And then we stayed in Washington for several days with the Schifflers at the Raleigh Hotel, and we went out to visit Admiral King at Bethesda. He was away at the time. Then we went out to visit Grosvenor of the Na...

Q: Gilbert Grosvenor?

Mrs. N.: Yes, Gilbert Grosvenor, and he gave me a very beautiful book on Kashmir that had been given to his wife years before. Oh, we got to know Mrs. Stone, the widow of Chief Justice Stone, very well in Washington, and we went to, oh, innumerable parties and things in that day or so that we were there. Then we left on the night of March 27th and took the train up to New York and arrived at Pennsylvania Station at 6 a.m., after a comfortable ride up. We were met by Signalman First Class White and a Marine Corporal who helped us with baggage. Also meeting us was Major Davis of the Marine Corps who belonged to the Military Staff Committee, who brought the messages from Vice Admiral Bieri, compliments and said he would be my aide while here. Well, it was cool and overcast. We went to live at the River Club on 52nd Street on the East River.

Q: That was a very fancy place, wasn't it?

Mrs. N.: Yes. We stayed there usually because of Paul Hammond. And he called on people and we went to - at 11 o'clock called on Secretary General of the UN, Mr. Trygve Lie, and his executive assistant, Andy Cordier. Both are very pleasant and we got busy at once discussing the organization of the plebescite administration for Kashmir and the staffing of it. Met many of the men who are under consideration. Dr. Wambaugh, who is an expert on plebescites matters. I lunched with Cordier and other guests. Byron Price, the U.S. budget - UN budget, officer - and Wesley Adams, a State Department representative who was helping us. Got home at 7 p.m., just in time to dress for Paul Hammond's dinner, at which we met Mr. and Mrs. Harrison. He's the architect working on the new UN building, and...

Q: Was that his first relationship with Paul Hammond or...?

Mrs. N.: No, no. He'd known him all through the war and I guess even before the war he met him. Then we were in New York, and he met a great many people and worked. We went to a dinner where we met Elihu Root and Mrs. Somebody-or-other - he left this blank, I don't know just why - and Mr. and Mrs. Radziwill. Oh yes, "We plan to stay until Monday morning when we will return to New York." Oh, then he says, oh yes, we had made arrangements to go back to Washington for a while and then, "we'll stay in Washington until Monday morning when we return to New York." Then he had a meeting in Washington and came out very depressed because he had hoped to take over to Kashmir to run this election with him, Navy people, those that had just retired or something like that, that he knew and unfortunately the Navy said they can't be given any pay. They lose their Navy pay. Chester was in a different status.

Q: He was five stars.

Mrs N.: Well, no, because he was at the head of this mission. They looked it up and they had the Supreme Court, I think, say whether he could have extra pay or not. And they did. The

State Department paid him - I mean the UN paid him, and because that was not an American organization, he could get it, but the others were coming in under the American group, so they couldn't get it. Then he found that he was to take different people from different countries. His staff was to be made up of all kinds, and he began arranging it. He quickly found that he was going to have a very excellent staff, and he conferred with Major General Harry J. Maloney, USA, Retired. He just was retiring on April 1st or the 30th of March. And he agreed to serve as Deputy PlebAd, that's what they called this plebescite, and "at 5 called on the foreign minister of Pakistan, Zafrulla Khan, at the Berkeley Hotel in New York, he having just arrived and having changed his itinerary to New York just to meet me. He is a dynamic person with great capacity. He is a most enchanting person.

Q: Yes, I've met him.

Mrs. N.: Very fond of him. Speaks beautiful English and with great fluency and rapidity. "Had a cup of tea with him. Quiet dinner at the River Club where the Hammonds joined after we had nearly finished, and about 9.30 Mr. Ross on Senator Austin's staff at the UN, and Mr.   from the State Department joined us, and at 10.40 we all left for the station to return to our respective destinations. We turned in at 1 in the Washington train and had a good night's rest." So this is the way it started at the United Nations, and there is a very great deal, many books of what we had to do getting ready for this, and there was a plane just sitting on the ground waiting for us to go to India when we discover that there was a fly in the ointment, that Nehru discovered that all of his men liked Chester trenendously and that the Pakistanis all liked Chester tremendously, and that the newspapers were all excited over his coming out, and Ithink Nehru began to figure that if the plebescite took place at that time, Pakistan would definitely be the winner, and he wanted no part of it, and he would never make the final OK that would get us off the ground. And after a very short time - it didn't take Chester too long to sense that this was going to happen and he suggested to the UN that instead of paying him this big salary, let him go back. They said, you stay here. We'll let your staff go, but we've got a lot of use for you, and they tried all that time to get it streightened out, but he was there at the United Nations for about two years, and he did a great many things, and he worked on this proposition all the time.

Q: But Nehru postponed it all that time?

Mrs. N. Nehru hasn't yet agreed to it. He had not when he died.

Miss N.: Yes, remember there was at least one other administrator...

Mrs. N.: Yes, he was a man who had been President of North Carolina...

Miss N.: Yes. he was President of North Carolina - Dr. Frank Somebody-or-other, who was there and he...

Mrs. N.: Just twiddled his thumbs.

Mrs. and Miss Nimitz - 38

Miss N.: ...hung on a string for a while and, I think...

Q: Was that Gray?

Miss N.: No, not Gray, what was his name, er, sorry, it's slipped my mind...

Mrs. N.: I can't think of it and I haven't got it here, but...

Miss N.: Oh, there's one person, it occurs to me that Mr. Mason might like to talk to and that is a young Englishman, the former Indian Army officer who was on his staff..

Mrs. N.: Yes. I think he's on an island off England, don't you?

Miss N.: What was his name, Mother?

Mrs. N.: His name was Anthony Bates - B-e-y-t-s. Major Anthony Beyts. He'd been born in India before it was separated - India and Pakistan - and he'd done mostof his soldiering up in Pakistan area and had terrific admiration for the Pakistanis. He was a great help to Chester because he knew that country so thoroughly, and...

Q: I suppose the United Nations people could give me a line on him - on his whereabouts?

Mrs. N.: Well, I doubt if they can now because it's been so many years. But I tell you where I think you could find it. Perhaps from a British consulate, or from the State Department.

Miss N.: Yes, because he is - he does occupy some position in the British ~~parliament~~ foreign service.

Mrs. N.: Well, I tell you what - not too long ago, or rather, it was long ago - Chester died in February and I went East in June and because of the airplane strike was held up some time. When I got back at the end of August, the first thing I saw was a letter from an Air Force officer - Major somebody - and I thought "what is this?" And I opened it and he enclosed a letter from Anthony Beyts, and Tony was on the island of Argentia.

Q: Argentia?

Mrs. N.: Argentia - down in North Africa, you know.

Q: No, it's up in Newfoundland.

Mrs. N.: It isn't Argentia. It's...

Q: Madagascar?

Mrs. N.: No, it's a very - its and island where we have an...

Q: Mauritius?

Mrs. N.: No. It begins with A, and it's an island - give me the atlas. I can find it.

Q: Is it an atoll down there - Atkins?

Mrs. N.: No. No. no. Anyway, he said "I'm the governor of this island," and he said the United States Air Force said they'd be delighted to fly you down here and come and stay with us for a while. Well, I'd just gotten back and I knew I couldn't do it but you know it was one of those things that gave me a terrific lift when I felt that the exciting things were over for me, to suddenly have an invitation to be flown by an Air Force plane to this island...

Q: In the middle of the Indian Ocean.

Mrs. N.: Yes. Wait a minute. It's off of Africa.

Q: Reunion? There's an island - what is that, Reunion Island?

Mrs. N.: No, this is somewhere off of...

Mrs. and Miss Nimitz - 40

Miss N.: Is it in the Indian Ocean, Mother?

Mrs. N.: Yes. Wait a minute. It is - oh, it's where - I'd never heard of it and I had to rush to this book and look it up.

Q: Ascension is all I...

Mrs. N.: Wait a minute - Ascension? That's it. Ascension Island..

Q: Well, that certainly is in the middle of nowhere.

Mrs. N. It is, and I thought, of course, it was terribly exciting, so I wrote Tony and said that I'd gotten it two months later than I should have and that - he said in the thing that they were leaving there in September - so I wrote him and said that I couldn't come, but I certainly was thrilled to get the invitation because I thought it would have been quite wonderful to go out there. But he was a very enthusiastic person and his youngest son is named for Chester. He's Chester Nimitz Beyts.

Miss N.: Well.

Mrs. N.: He had a charming wife.

Q: Did you go to New York when he was with the United Nations?

Miss N.: I was studying in the Regional Studies Program in Cambridge at the time and I did go down one, I think, one spring or one fall, I've forgotten which, when you were living at the BOQ ...

Mrs. N.: You see, when we first went there, to the United Nations, and the United Nations was at Lake Success, Marion Eppley, who was a captain in the Naval Reserve, and his wife

Mrs. and Miss Nimitz - 41

had a beautiful place at Oyster Bay and they insisted that we come out and stay with them. So we did for a month - much to - I'm not a visitor and I must say it was very difficult many times, but we were very fond of Marion Appley. He was very easy. His wife was a sort of - I didn't learn until afterwards that she had never liked Navy people, so this was sort of tough on her and I really thought it was awfully tough on her, and I was studying Hindi at that time, so I spent a great deal of time up in my room studying during the day, and they had a beautiful pier and I'd go swimming every little while, and she was busy with the yard or she would go off and do things, and we would lunch together. We always had a very pleasant time together, but we hadn't very much in common. We stayed there a month because they wouldn't let us go, and then at the end of a month we had an invitation to live at Sands Point in that program that they have there for - it was some - well it was when they were starting programs of using this radio business and having an instructor somewhere and having the thing piped into places...

Q: Oh, yes.

Mrs. N.: Yes, and all sorts of...

Q: Closed circuit.

Mrs. N.: Yes, and then they had a lot of other things they did. I don't remember exactly. Special devices, that's what it was. The special devices centre. Anyway, they had this - they had rented for this bachelor officers' quarters and for the commanding officers' quarters, this magnificent estate which had been brought over, piece by piece, from England and set up there, and we were invited to live there. Well, that was a perfect set-up because it meant we were not bothering anybody. We had a suite of rooms and we ate with the bachelor officers. So we lived there for quite a while, and that was when we got to know the Cushmans and the Wheelers, because we spent a great deal of time with both of those people. Then when we moved up to New York, when they opened the UN at New York, I think it was either then or - yes, it was - no, it was when we first went up to New York before we went out to live with the Cushmans, with the Eppleys, we had - we were invited to live with the Tom Watsons...

Q: The IBM people?

Mrs. N.: IBM. Senior Tom Watsons, and Tom and Jeanette and Chester and I had a marvelous month together and they were awfully hurt when we insisted on going to a hotel to live, because we felt that there was a limit on how long people may stay because we found we weren't going to India right away. And, oh, they felt so badly over it. They'd come and pick us up and we'd go up to Endicott and we'd go all around with them. So we had a very delightful lot of friends who did a great deal for us at the UN. We enjoyed the United Nations people very much indeed, and we went to all kinds of parties given by the different delegations, and we always at luncheon in the UN - we never could lunch alone, we always had someone who would come up - Malik from Lebanon would come and have lunch with us, Andy Cordier, and Ralph Bunche came frequently, and a lot of the other people who were going out on this expedition with us would come and have lunch.

Q: Who was the senior U.S. representative - Warren Austin?

Mrs. N.: Warren Austin was the senior one, and I always loved Mrs. Austin because I could always tell where she was because she had a bright red hat that she wore. And if I saw a bright red hat, I'd know I could always find Mrs. Warren Austin.

Q: And this was at the time when Eleanor Roosevelt was attached to the United Nations?

Mrs. N.: Yes, we saw a great deal of her and admired her tremendously. She was a very great power for good in that organization. We felt that she did a - just a super job.

Q: You must tell me that story you told yesterday - the story that your daughter, Mary, wanted you to tell, the dinner with Gromyko.

Mrs. N.: Well, I think that - you check that with Cordier - to be sure I have it entirely correct before I tell you that.

Q: But he wouldn't know all the details that you related yesterday.

Mrs. N.: Well...

Q: About the flowers and...

Mrs. N.: Well, we were told that we were invited to this dinner at Trygve Lie's house, and it was at a time when our relations with Russia were definitely strained and when there was the Berlin blockade. When we got to the dinner party, which was a very formal one, my husband came to me as I came out of the ladies' coat room and said, "Do you know who your dinner partner's going to be?" and I said, "Well, is it going to be Gromyko?" and he said, "Yes, it is." I said, "Well, I think I can get on with Gromyko very well." So when I went in to dinner, Mr. Gromyko was standing there waiting to pull my chair out for me, and I spoke to him, and as he sat down I turned to him and said, "Let's drink a toast to peace," and he said, "Let's." And we drank a toast to peace, and I began asking him whether Mrs. Gromyko was coming and he said in a rather pained and tired voice, which made me realize that everybody had been asking him this and he had taken it - because he had always asnwered that she wasn't coming - that they thought it was because he didn't trust people over here or something, and he remarked that no, she wasn't coming because their son was to go into the university in Moscow the next year and that our prep schools in this country were so entirely different from what he would need to go into this Russian school that she had to stay there and help him study and have a place for him to come to. And I immediately told Mr. Gromyko that I understood that absolutely, because many was the time when I had to give up being with Chester because the children were getting ready for college or in high school and couldn't be moved. So I said this I'm very sympathetic with, and then we talked about our families, and about this time Mr. Trygve Lie broke in because I was sitting on Mr. Lie's left and Gromyko was sitting on my left, and Mr Lie started talking business to Mr. Gromyko, and Mr. Gromyko immediately clammed up and became very annoyed and finally he said to Mr.

Lie, "Let us not talk business at dinner," and, I think feeling no pain, I said to Mr. Gromyko - Mr. Trygve Lie - "No, let's not talk business at dinner. Let's talk about music and flowers." Gromyko let out a sigh and said "yes, let's," and Mr. Lie looked at me and laughed and turned away and started talking to the person on the other side. So I asked Mr. Gromyko which he knew most about, flowers or music, and he said, "neither." And I said, "Well, then, I will proceed to tell you some good Navy stories," which I did.

Q: Were they some of your husband's best?

Mrs. N.: Yes, they were some of the best, and when we separated at the end of dinner, the ladies went into a room and the gentlemen disappeared somewhere at the upper part of the house. Well, it seemed they would never come down. The ladies were all ready to go to bed. It was 12 o'clock. It was 12.30, and this dinner had started by 7, so finally the men came down and we went out and went home. And we were talking about our experiences and the driver was our Marine Cozard and he was talking about his experiences, because all the UN drivers were from all countries all over the world, and Cozard was a very convivial person, and they'd all been sitting out there talking all the chauffeurs together for these five hours, and finally they looked over and saw the Russian chauffeurs off by themselves. So Cozard went over to see if they'd come and join them, and they said very quietly they weren't allowed to. So he went back and a few days later I was at the UN and we were lunching together and Andy Cordier came in, and I said, "Oh, Andy, I didn't have any difficulty with Gromyko. We got on beautifully." And Andy looked at me with a funny look on his face, and he said, "Well, you think we weren't watching you. You were put there for that purpose." And, he said, "We were watching you very clo-sely," and he said after a minute or two of talking about it, "It might interest you to know that on that night we took Gromyko upstairs after dinner and we broke the Berlin blockade." Which I've always thought was very pleasant.

Q: The Navy stories had an influence - that's the inference.

Mrs. N.: I don't know how much influence.

How about some sherry now?

Miss N.: Yes.

Mrs. N.: One amusing thing: we were invited to a reception given by the Venezuelan organization, and Venezuela, from my point of view, all of their parties - they always asked at least ten times more than could possibly get into the house, and people were always wandering around the streets trying to find a place to stand.

Q: Maybe they have the expectation that they won't be accepted.

Mrs. N.: No, they want to get it all over at once.

Miss N.: There are people other than the Venezuelans who occasionally do the same thing.

Mrs. N.: Well, anyway, at this particular party, they had a

small apartment in New York, and Chester and I went up in the elevator and we got out of the elevator - there wasn't a place for anything there - but we finally wormed our way in a little bit, long enough to make our presence known, and then we just slid out toward the door. As we got out to the corridor, I think it was the representative of Byelorussia (sp) who had been so damnable at the UN all the time, he was agin everything and he came in - he had just gotten out of the elevator - and he was looking around. There was no place to put anything - just this very small apartment with this small shelf - and he had just tried to put his hat up on the shelf and the hat started to fall down. Well, he and I both recognized at the same moment if it ever got on the floor it was gone. So he was hunting in one direction and I was hunting in another. Well, I caught the hat and I tried to put my two hands together to grab this hat and, lo and behold, he stepped back at that moment and I slammed his hat into his face - I just slammed it there - and, do you know, I thought I had it between my two hands, I opened my hands with sort of qualms as to what would happen and he looked at me and I looked at him, and we both burst out laughing because we both realized that the hat was saved. If it had ever gotten to the floor, he couldn't have leaned down to pick it up. So that was the only time I ever in my two years there - round the United Nations - saw that man anything but disagreeable. And after I came down I said to somebody after I got there, "I bet I'm the only woman in this country who's slammed his hat into his face and gotten a smile for doing it."

Q: You say that there are seven or eight schools named in honor of the Admiral?

Miss N.: Yes. There is one down on the Peninsula, an elementary school. I have a picture that was taken by a news photographer one day when Mother and Daddy went down to visit the school, and it is just enchanting. He is sitting with, I gather, at least several grades of kids sort of arranged behind him in a semicircle, and he is just beaming from ear to ear and most of the children's faces in this picture are also, you know, sort of split with grins. It is just a very disarming picture.

Q: You say this is a fact that all these schools were named for him - his name associated with education was a great bang to him?

Miss N.: Oh,..

Mrs. N.: There's a new Nimitz facility for the University of California. It is the oceanography thing at the entrance to San Diego. I just got a letter from them the other day and I'm wondering if I ever answered it.

Q: Wasn't he, in the last years, wasn't he associated actively with the subject of oceanography?

Mrs. N.: No. Mary is the oceanographer.

Miss N.: He was interested but I think quite a few checks were sent to establish a scholarship at the time he died for somebody who was going to the...

Mrs. N.: Now, this is a tribute written by Robert Anderson, whose name we gave you, when Chester died. He knew him very well. But the one I wanted was a little paper, I can't see it here. Here's that poem that I read to you.

Q: May I read this into the tape?

Miss N.: Yes. Go ahead.

Q: This is an editorial from the San Diego Union on Tuesday, July 25, 1967. Memoriam in Sea Power, it's titled:

USS Nimitz is perfect tribute. Selection of the name USS Nimitz for the next nuclear aircraft carrier in the U.S. is not only an honor to the family of the late fleet admiral, it's a tribute to the Navy and nation. "Uncommon valor became a common virtue" said the late fleet admiral during the dark days of World War II as he assessed the magnificent performance of the Allied fighting men. It was a phrase that became a classic for all time to describe the performance of our men when the nation calls for their services. It also is a phrase that can be aptly applied to Admiral Nimitz, who commanded the Allied troops in the Pacific during the war. His also was uncommon valor, not only during World War II but throughout sixty-three illustrious years of serice to his nation through the Navy. Nimitz is a proud name. It will live forever in the annals of the Navy and the nation as an example of leadership, patriotism, and as a beacon for others to emulate. As a nation we cannot pay the debt we owe to Admiral Nimitz, but we can and should pay him the highest and most appropriate honor. Nothing can be more appropriate than naming the next nuclear carrier Nimitz. It is a proud name for a proud ship. It is eminently appropriate. To the day of his death when he still was in the service of his nation, Admiral Nimitz believed in the value of unconquerable sea power. Not just men and ships, but sea power of the kind that continues to grow to meet the strategic needs of the times. The carrier Nimitz will be the epitome of sea power, it will be, when finished, about 1972, the strongest fighting ship afloat and the most mighty in history. It will represent the nuclear Navy of the future. As Mrs. Nimitz said, upon learning of the honor, "Chester Nimitz knew that our national strength is in the leadership of the naval stature to have what is to be the latest development of sea power laid down in his memory is to have for him the perfect tribute." Admiral Nimitz was a man of quiet dignity, but a man of strength. He also was a man of peace but one who knew that only the strong persons and nations can have peace. The USS Nimitz will symbolize all of these. It is fitting and proper that a proud nation should name its proudest ship after one of its proudest exponents of sea power."

and this was written by whom?

Miss N.: Captain Robert Anderson

Q: ...that's almost an adage on self-reliance.

Miss N.: Well, there was an expression which the old man either coined himself or which he encountered somewhere and which evidently struck him very forcefully, and which he reported to me that he had used in an address to some visiting school ship which had midshipmen on it.

Mrs. N.: It's the Almirante Saldanus [Sardonis] from Brazil [Portugal].

Miss N.: From Brazil, that's right, and he apparently at one point in his speech had said that when the time comes that you think you need a helping hand, look on the end of your own right arm, which implies that one should, you know, exhaust one's own resources, and yet he himself was certainly the first invariably to proffer help and to say whenever he called or whenever I called the house, "What can we do for you?"

Mrs. N.: Well, here's a prayer which - this was the Admiral's favorite prayer. He did not write it. Someone p-rinted that he had written it. He did not.

> "God grant me the courage to change the things that I can change, the serenity to accept those I cannot change, and the wisdom to know the difference. But, God, grant me the courage not to give up on what I think is right, even though I think it is hopeless."

INDEX

for an interview

with

MRS. CHESTER AND MISS NANCY NIMITZ

Acheson, Dean Gooderham and Mrs., 33

Adams, Wesley, 35

Almirante Saldanus, 51

Anderson, E. Robert, 48, 50

Aquinas, Mary (Nimitz) 31

Ascension Island, 39-40

Austin, Senator Warren and Mrs., 36, 43

Berkeley, 20-24

Beyts, Major Anthony, 38-39

Bieri, Admiral Bernhard H., 34

Buckley, Mr., 29

Bunche, Ralph, 42

California, University of, 18-19, 23, 27, 48

Canaga, Bruce and Elizabeth, 32

Clark, Dr. Gale, 9-11

Cordier, Dr. Andrew, 32, 34-35, 42-43

Cozard, George E., 33, 45-46

Cushman, Mr. and Mrs. E. Sanderson, 42

Davis, Major, 34

Denfeld, Admiral Louis E., 29

Eppley, Captain Marion, 40-42

Final, 6

Geneva Convention, 2

Gromyko, Andrei A., 43-46

Grosvenor, Gilbert, 34

Gunther, Commander Ernest, 21-22

Hammond, Paul, 34-36

Harrison, Mr. and Mrs., 35

Hoover, President Herbert, 25-26

Hueneme, Port, 31

Japan, 2, 5-6

Khan, Zafrulla, 36

King, Admiral Ernest J., 34

Lattu, Admiral Onnie P., 19-20

Lay, Catherine (Nimitz) 7, 12

Leahy, Admiral William D., 33

Lerschner, 24-25

Lie, Secretary General Trygve, 32, 34, 43-45

Lusitania, 26

Malik, Charles Habib, 42

Maloney, Major General Harry J., 36

Manhattan Project, 5

McCoy, Major General Frank, 33

Missouri, 6

Nehru, Pandit Jawaharial, 37

The New Scientist, 2

USS *Nimitz*, 49-50

Nimitz, Catherine, (see Lay) ~~7, 12~~

Nimitz, Chester Jr., and Joan, 3, 29, 31-32

Nimitz, Mary (see Aquinas)

NROTC, 19, 22, 24

Nuclear weapons, 1, 5-6

Page, Lieutenant, 33

Price, Byron, 35

Radziwill, Mr. and Mrs., 35

Robison, Admiral S. S., 29-30

Roosevelt, Eleanor, 43

Roosevelt, President Franklin D., 2

Root, Elihu, 35

Ross, John Claudius, 36

Rusk, Secretary Dean, 30

San Diego Union, 49

Schifflers, Mr. and Mrs. Kurt C., 32, 34

Scientific American, 2

Stone, Mrs. Clyde Ernest, 34

Sullivan, Secretary John Lawrence, 32

Thomson, Lieutenant, 32-33

United Nations, 28-42

Wambaugh, Dr., 35

Wambaugh, Sarah, 33

Watsons, Tom and Jeanette, 42

Wheeler, Mr. and Mrs. Joe, 42

White, Signalman, 34

Woods, Dean, 27

Wooldridge, Admiral Edmund Tyler, 30, 32

www.ingramcontent.com/pod-product-compliance
Lightning Source LLC
Chambersburg PA
CBHW080611170426
43209CB00007B/1398